AN USBORNE GUIDE
HAIR
& HAIRSTYLING

Paula Woods

Edited by Felicity Everett
Designed by Nerissa Davies

Illustrated by Tessa Land, Peter Bull, Joanna Irving and Paul Sullivan

Photographs courtesy of Vidal Sassoon and The Kobal Collection

Additional designs by Christopher Gillingwater

Additional research by Sarah Caughlin

Contents

About hair and hairstyling

A new hairstyle can change your appearance radically. A successful one can improve your looks and lift your spirits. An unsuccessful one can make you reluctant to leave the house. Because of this, most people are prepared to spend quite large amounts of money having their hair done in a flattering style, and to devote the time to keeping it in good condition afterwards.

This book is about choosing and looking after your hairstyle. It is also an introduction to the world of hairdressing, for those with a passing interest in the tricks of the trade, or a serious ambition to become stylists themselves.

Pages 3–21 cover everything you need to know as a client, from choosing the right style to tips on looking after your hair on a daily basis and ways to vary your chosen style for a special occasion or on vacation. This section of the book is indicated with a purple flash at the top of each page for easy reference.

Pages 22-47 are about the world of the professional hairstylist. This section tells you all about the equipment they need and gives a clear, step-by-step guide to the basic cutting, perming and coloring techniques that a trainee hairdresser has to learn. This section is indicated with a green flash at the top of each page.

At the back of the book there is lots of down-to-earth careers advice on hairdressing and related fields. There is also some suggested reading and useful addresses, should you want to find out more about becoming a hairdresser.

How hair grows

The hair on your head is there for two reasons: to stop your body from losing heat, and to protect your scalp (and therefore your brain) from injury. Here you can find out about the structure of your scalp and hair.

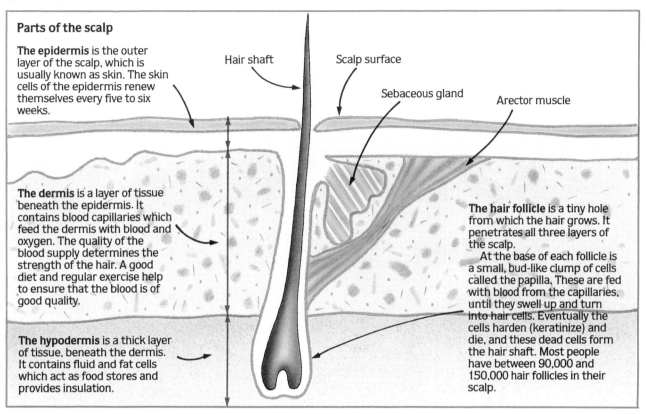

Parts of the scalp

The epidermis is the outer layer of the scalp, which is usually known as skin. The skin cells of the epidermis renew themselves every five to six weeks.

Hair shaft

Scalp surface

Sebaceous gland

Arector muscle

The dermis is a layer of tissue beneath the epidermis. It contains blood capillaries which feed the dermis with blood and oxygen. The quality of the blood supply determines the strength of the hair. A good diet and regular exercise help to ensure that the blood is of good quality.

The hypodermis is a thick layer of tissue, beneath the dermis. It contains fluid and fat cells which act as food stores and provides insulation.

The hair follicle is a tiny hole from which the hair grows. It penetrates all three layers of the scalp.

At the base of each follicle is a small, bud-like clump of cells called the papilla. These are fed with blood from the capillaries, until they swell up and turn into hair cells. Eventually the cells harden (keratinize) and die, and these dead cells form the hair shaft. Most people have between 90,000 and 150,000 hair follicles in their scalp.

Cross section of a hair shaft

Medulla

Cortex

Cuticle

A hair shaft consists of three layers:

The medulla is the core of the hair shaft. It is a soft, spongy layer of round cells. The size of these cells determines the thickness of your hair.

The cortex is an inner layer made up of cells which give the hair elasticity and strength. It also contains a pigment* called melanin, which gives the hair its color.

The cuticle is a protective coating made up of clear, overlapping scales of keratin (a horn like substance). If you look after your hair, these scales should lie flat, making the surface of the hair look glossy.

The life cycle of a hair

Each hair lives between one and six years. It then dies and falls out of the hair follicle (see above).

Every day, between 50 and 150 hairs die, but new ones are constantly growing to take their place, so the hair loss is not noticeable.

There are three phases in the life cycle of a hair: the anogen phase, the telogen phase and the catogen phase. You can find out more about them on the right.

The **anogen phase** is the period of new growth. Most people's hair grows at a rate of about 1.3cm a month. The sebaceous glands are active throughout this phase. At any one time, 18% of your hair is in the anogen phase.

During the **telogen phase** growth stops and the sebaceous glands become less active. Only 1% of your hair is at this stage at any one time.

The **catogen phase** is the final one. The sebaceous glands stop working and the follicle shrinks. After about three months, the hair falls out. About 4 to 14% of hair is at this stage at any one time.

* Pigment is a special name for the chemicals which give color to your hair and skin.

Hair types

Before styling your hair, a good hairdresser will examine it carefully to see what type it is. For example, how thick is it? What is its natural color? Is it greasy or dry? Doing this helps the hairdresser to make the most of your hair.

Below you can see why people have such different types of hair.

Thick or thin?

The thickness of your hair depends on the number of hair follicles* you have and how large each individual follicle is.

Blonds have the most hair follicles but because each hair is so fine, they appear to have the thinnest hair. Redheads, on the other hand, have the fewest hair follicles but owing to the thickness of each hair, they seem to have a lot of hair.

Hair color

The color of your hair is determined by a colored substance (called a pigment) within each hair shaft*. If you look closely you will see that although your hair has an overall shade, the individual hairs vary quite considerably.

You can change your natural shade by using a colorant (see pages 34-35). It is a good idea to choose a shade which is fairly close to your own, as this will probably suit your skin tone best.

Hair length

Whether or not you can wear your hair long depends on its growth rate and resilience. On average, each hair grows 1.3cm per month and continues growing for between two and six years. After this it falls out.

If your hair grows at an above average rate for five years or more, you will be able to choose a long hairstyle. If you have slow-growing or weak hair, you will probably not be able to grow it past your shoulders.

Hair follicles

As explained on page 3, your hair grows from tiny holes in your head, called follicles. The shape of these holes effect how curly your hair is. Their size determines whether it is thick or thin.

Small follicles

Small follicles produce fine hair. If you have fine hair, avoid rich conditioners as these make it soft and limp. To add body to your hair, try having it permed (see pages 38-39).

Large follicles

Large follicles result in thick hair. This can be stubborn to style and takes a long time to dry, but has the advantage of natural body.

See page 3 for more about hair follicles and hair shafts.

Round follicles

A round follicle produces straight hair. You can curl it temporarily in various ways (see pages 36-37).

Asian hair will hold a perm better and for much longer than any other type of straight hair. This is because the cuticle (see right) is particularly strong and thick.

Kidney-shaped follicles

A kidney-shaped follicle makes the hair kink, and appear curly or wavy. The more acute the shape, the curlier the hair. You can straighten curly hair using perming lotion (see page 39) or heated straighteners (see page 45).

Afro Caribbean hair not only grows from a kidney-shaped follicle, but each shaft is oval in shape rather than round. This combination produces tighter curls.

An advantage of Afro Caribbean hair is that the curls protect the head from the sun's rays by absorbing them at varying angles. However, they also allow moisture to escape and prevent the natural oil from coating the hair shaft, so the hair is very often dry.

Shiny hair

How shiny your hair is depends on how well each hair shaft is able to reflect light. By keeping your hair in good condition you will ensure that the protective coating (the cuticle) of each hair shaft lies flat, as shown on the right. This creates a smooth surface which reflects light well.

Healthy cuticle: Scales lie flat and overlap creating a smooth surface to reflect light.

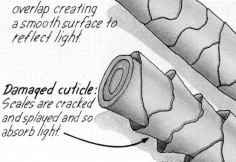

Damaged cuticle: Scales are cracked and splayed and so absorb light.

Dry, greasy or normal?

Hair follicles contain sebaceous glands (see page 3) which produce oil to keep the hair healthy. However some produce too much, or too little oil, which can lead to your hair becoming greasy or dry.

This chart will help you identify your particular hair condition, and provides tips on looking after it. For more advice on hair care, see page 17.

Hair condition	Appearance	Cause	Associated problems	Solution
Greasy	Hair becomes lank and dull after washing. Looks greasy.	Sebaceous glands are producing too much oil.	People with fine hair or oily skin are more likely to have greasy hair.	Wash frequently* with a very mild shampoo as extra oil attracts dirt.
Dry	Hair is hard to control and feels rough to the touch. Looks dull and brittle.	Sebaceous glands are not producing enough oil. Alternatively, hair has been damaged by careless treatment.	Split ends (see page 46) can be a problem. Dry hair is often accompanied by dry skin.	Use a rich, specially formulated shampoo. Condition after every wash.
Combination	Hair appears oily at the top and dry at the ends. Scalp may feel dry and flaky.	Often due to over-use of heated styling appliances which dry out the ends of the hair.	The hair may suffer from dandruff (see page 46) and split ends.	Use a mild shampoo and apply a rich oil-based conditioner to the ends of the hair only.
Normal	Hair is shiny and easy to manage. Feels soft and smooth to the touch.	Sebaceous glands are producing the correct amount of oil.	None	Use a mild shampoo and a conditioning rinse if necessary.

Frequent washing does not make hair more oily if you wash it carefully and with the right products.

Natural hair preparations

For generations, people have used herbal products to enhance their hair and skin. There are now many specialist shops which stock these products. However, you don't need to spend a fortune on them: much of what you need, such as lemons, oil and vinegar, can be found in the kitchen cupboard.

Before trying anything new, remember that even mild products, if over-used, can harm your hair. However, natural preparations used every so often will improve your hair.

On the right you can find out the properties of the different natural ingredients. Below are some recipes for shampoos and conditioners.

Cider Vinegar is a mild acid. As many hair products are slightly alkaline, a vinegar rinse can help correct the pH balance of your hair and scalp (see page 42). This gives the hair extra body and shine. After using vinegar, always rinse thoroughly to remove all traces of its distinctive smell.

Lemon juice closes the pores (tiny holes) in the scalp and helps smooth down the overlapping scales of the hair shaft (see page 5). This leaves the hair looking glossy and well cared for.

Mayonnaise combines the properties of eggs, oil and vinegar. Together they leave your hair beautifully conditioned and shiny.

Egg shampoo	Egg conditioner	Warm oil treatment	Mayonnaise conditioner

1. Vigorously beat together the white and yolk of an egg in a mixing bowl.	1. Separate the egg yolk from the white. Beat the yolk thoroughly: this makes it easier to apply.	1. Gently warm two tablespoons of oil in a saucepan. Then carefully massage it into your hair.	1. Mix a tablespoon of cider vinegar, an egg yolk and a pinch of sugar. Stir in eight tablespoons of olive oil.

2. Massage the mixture thoroughly into unwashed dry hair and leave for around five minutes.	2. Wash your hair, then dab on the yolk with a sponge. Comb through to distribute it evenly.	2. Wrap a piece of plastic wrap around your hair, and seal the ends by scrunching them together.	2. Beat vigorously until the mixture becomes thick and creamy, then bottle it and store it in the fridge.

3. Rinse your hair in *cool* water: the egg is likely to scramble if the water is too hot.	3. Leave for 20 minutes and then rinse your hair thoroughly in cool water. Style hair as normal.	3. Cover with a warm towel*, and leave on overnight. Shampoo and rinse thoroughly.	3. Apply the mayonnaise as you would a warm oil treatment** or use it instead of a conditioner.

* The heat from the towel causes moisture to build-up under the plastic wrap.
** Leave for at least 20 minutes before rinsing.

Olive oil coats the hair with a thin layer of oil. This smooths down the outer cuticles (see page 5), allowing the hair to reflect light more efficiently and appear healthy and shiny.

Eggs make excellent cleansers. They cling to the dirt and, when you rinse your hair, they drag it away with them. As eggs contain protein they also act as a conditioner, leaving dull, lifeless hair full of body and shine. After using an egg, you will need to rinse your hair more than once to remove all traces of it.

Common herbs and plants can be used to cure various problems and improve the condition of your hair. You can apply them in the form of an infusion (see below).

Astringents

Astringents such as lime, lemon and witch hazel help to close the pores in your scalp and stem the flow of natural oil. They are therefore particularly good for greasy hair.

WITCH HAZEL

To keep your hair free of grease in between washes, apply astringent to your scalp using cotton wool.

Quick rinses

Lemon rinse. Add four teaspoons of lemon juice to a bowl of cool water, and use as a final rinse.

Vinegar rinse. Add half a cup of cider vinegar to a litre of water and use as a final rinse.

Infusions

You can make a wide range of hair remedies by soaking herbs or plants in hot water. These are known as infusions. Natural infusions add body and shine to all hair types and also help keep your hair in excellent condition.

To make an infusion

1. Place 25g of your selected herbs (see the chart on the right) in a container, and pour over 300ml of boiling water.

2. Close the container and leave in a warm place for several hours. The longer the infusion is allowed to steep, the stronger the effect of your rinse. Then strain the liquid into an airtight jar.

3. Use the infusion as a final rinse or as a supplement to your shampoo or conditioner (add half of it to shampoo or a quarter to conditioner).

Herb/flower	Property
Camomile flowers	Lightens blond hair. Adds shine to dull hair.
Hollyhock flowers	Adds blueish tinge to white or grey hair.
Lavender	Removes excess oil.
Marigold petals	Soothes irritated scalps. Brightens red tones in auburn hair.
Nettles	Stimulates hair growth.
Parsley	Helps prevent dandruff.
Rosemary	Prevents static.
Sage	Darkens grey hair. Adds shine to dark hair.

Buying herbal products

If you do not want to make your own herbal remedies you could buy ready-made versions from pharmacies or health shops. Look out for the items described below.

Orris root

If you do not always have time to wash your hair, buy some powdered orris root. This makes an excellent dry shampoo. Brush a little through your hair to remove grease and stale smells. Keep brushing until all traces of the powder have gone.

Rhassoul mud

Rhassoul or Moroccan mud is powder which, when mixed with water, makes a good cleanser for greasy hair. You can also use it to treat dandruff. It is sometimes sold as a ready-made shampoo.

Henna wax

This is a colorless wax which makes an excellent conditioning treatment for all hair types. Mix the henna wax with hot water (as directed on the container) and massage into clean dry hair. Leave on for about 30 minutes, then rinse.

Healthy hair – inside and out

Keeping your hair in good condition is not just a matter of choosing the right shampoo. A good diet and plenty of exercise are essential to give your hair shine and vitality. It is also important to protect it from extremes of temperature, pollutants and so on. Here you can find out how to make sure your hair looks good all year round, indoors and out.

Health and diet

For your hair to stay healthy, your scalp must receive a regular supply of blood. This ensures that the sebaceous glands and hair follicles work efficiently. To help your circulation, take plenty of exercise and eat a balanced, nutritious diet.

A healthy diet should include:

Low fat proteins. These are found in white meat and fish.

Vitamins (A, B and C). Vitamin A is found in milk, butter, eggs and fresh fruit and vegetables. Wholefoods, such as oats and wheatgerm contain vitamin B. Raw vegetables, salads and fresh fruit are high in vitamin C.

Minerals (iron, calcium and salt). These are found in liver, kidneys and vegetables.

You can also take vitamin supplements:

★ Yeast extracts such as brewers' yeast (which come in tablet or powder form), zinc or vitamin A tablets will improve the overall condition of your hair.

★ Brewers' yeast may also help if you find you are losing more hair than normal.

★ A daily course of vitamin E oil capsules may help if your hair is dry and brittle.

★ Kelp is a seaweed rich in vitamins and minerals. A course of tablets will strengthen and improve the condition of your hair.

Summer hair care

Summer usually makes you feel cheerful and energetic, which is good for your general health and therefore your hair. However it is important to be aware of the potentially harmful effects of summer weather and activities.

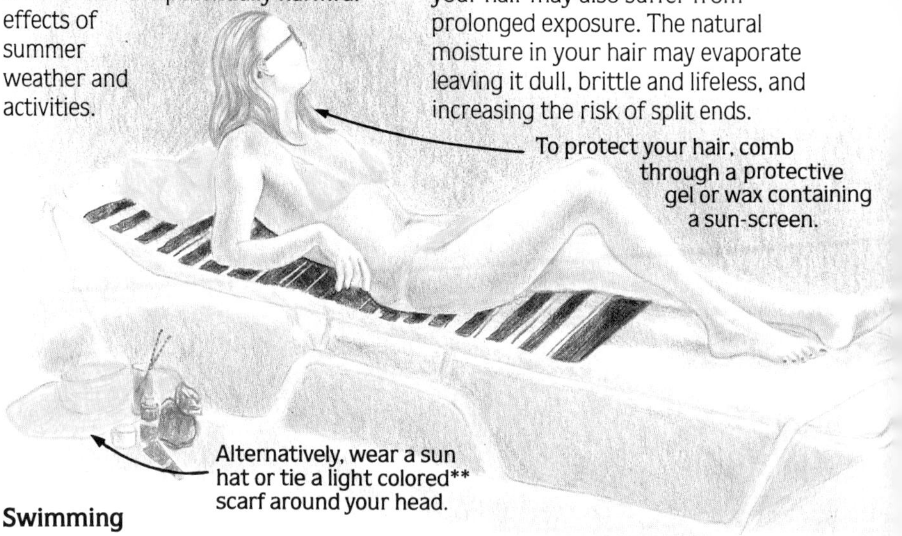

To protect your hair, comb through a protective gel or wax containing a sun-screen.

Alternatively, wear a sun hat or tie a light colored** scarf around your head.

Swimming

Swimming, whether in the sea or a swimming pool, can be damaging to your hair. If possible rinse your hair afterwards to remove any salt water or chlorine, both of which leave harmful deposits and spoil your hair's condition.

Summer breezes

Warm winds increase the drying effects of the sun. Sea breezes often contain grains of sand which tear your hair leaving it frizzy and unkempt. Hair gel or a scarf will give better protection than a sun hat, which is likely to blow off.

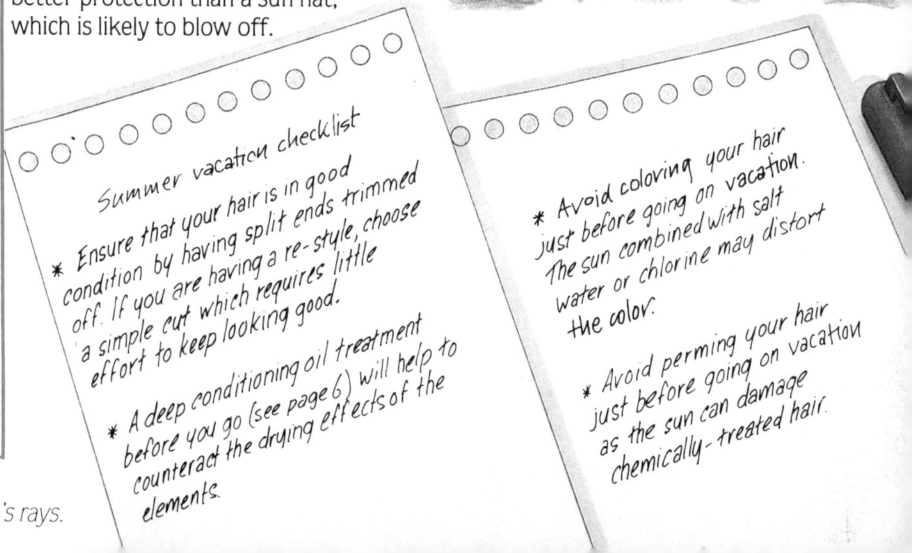

The sun

Exposure to the sun lightens most hair types. This can look very attractive with a tan. However, just as too much sun can damage your skin, your hair may also suffer from prolonged exposure. The natural moisture in your hair may evaporate leaving it dull, brittle and lifeless, and increasing the risk of split ends.

Always re-apply gels and waxes after swimming.

Summer vacation checklist

★ Ensure that your hair is in good condition by having split ends trimmed off. If you are having a re-style, choose a simple cut which requires little effort to keep looking good.

★ A deep conditioning oil treatment before you go (see page 6) will help to counteract the drying effects of the elements.

★ Avoid coloring your hair just before going on vacation. The sun combined with salt water or chlorine may distort the color.

★ Avoid perming your hair just before going on vacation as the sun can damage chemically-treated hair.

* These are taken internally.
** Light colors will reflect the sun's rays.

Winter hair care

In winter, it is not only the weather which can cause problems for your hair but the constant changes in temperature as you move between the cold outdoors and warm indoors.

You should always wear a hat when skiing.

The cold

Severe cold and sudden changes in temperature can make your hair brittle and dry. Always wear a hat or scarf out of doors to protect your hair as well as to keep you warm.

The wind

If you let your hair blow loose in the winter wind, you may end up with dry hair which is prone to split ends. Long hair may also become tangled and you could harm it trying to comb out the knots. To protect it, wear it tied back or cover it with a hat or scarf.

Snow, rain and mist

Moisture in the air, in the form of rain, snow and mist can make your hair frizzy, lifeless and unmanageable. This is because it reduces the effectiveness of styling products, such as hairsprays and gels. It will also take the body and shape out of styled hair.

Whilst an umbrella will protect you from bad snow and rain showers, light drizzle and mist can be all-pervasive. It may well be a waste of time curling or straightening your hair in this weather.

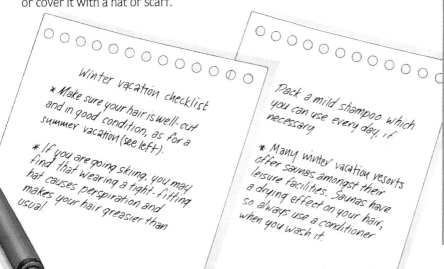

Winter vacation checklist
* Make sure your hair is well-cut and in good condition, as for a summer vacation (see left).

* If you are going skiing, you may find that wearing a tight-fitting hat causes perspiration and makes your hair greasier than usual.

Pack a mild shampoo which you can use every day, if necessary

* Many winter vacation resorts offer saunas amongst their leisure facilities. Saunas have a drying effect on your hair, so always use a conditioner when you wash it.

City haircare

If you move to a large town or city you may find that you need to wash your hair more often. This is because of the additional dirt in the air. It is best to change to a mild or frequent-wash shampoo. You may also find your hair difficult to manage. This is due to pollution in the air which affects the acid balance* of your hair. There is little you can do to prevent this, although using a pH balanced shampoo and conditioning your hair regularly may help.

Protecting the environment

Many everyday styling products come in aerosol sprays. These harm the atmosphere because they contain chlorofluorocarbons (CFC's). When you use an aerosol spray you release these chemicals into the atmosphere. They slowly destroy the earth's ozone layer (the layer of gas which filters out ultra-violet radiation from the sun).

Many companies now produce pump-action sprays, which are an effective alternative.

Indoor hair care

Home comforts, such as central heating or artificially purified and softened water, make life more enjoyable, but can cause problems for your hair. You can find out what these are and how to tackle them below.

Heating

Most home heating systems, and central heating in particular, evaporate the moisture from the air. This has a drying effect on your hair. You can replace some of the air's moisture by placing a bowl of water in each room of the house. Make sure they cannot easily be knocked over.

Tap water

In hard-water areas the water supply is often supplemented with fluoride and chlorine which purifies and softens the water, but is bad for your hair. If there are such chemicals in your water, make sure you condition your hair after shampooing.

* See page 42.

Choosing the right style

Have you ever found a picture of a hairstyle you would like and taken it along to your hairdresser only to be advised against it? This is often because of your hair type and texture (see pages 4-5), but the hairdresser will also consider your face shape and features. A good hairdresser will help you choose a style which flatters the way you look. This involves deciding which features to emphasize and which to disguise. On these two pages you can find out what shape your face is and which styles might suit you.

Over the page are some tips on emphasizing your best features and choosing a cut to suit your lifestyle.

Face shapes

Once you have identified the shape of your face using the method shown on the opposite page, you can work out what sort of style might suit you. Here are some tips for the six basic face shapes.

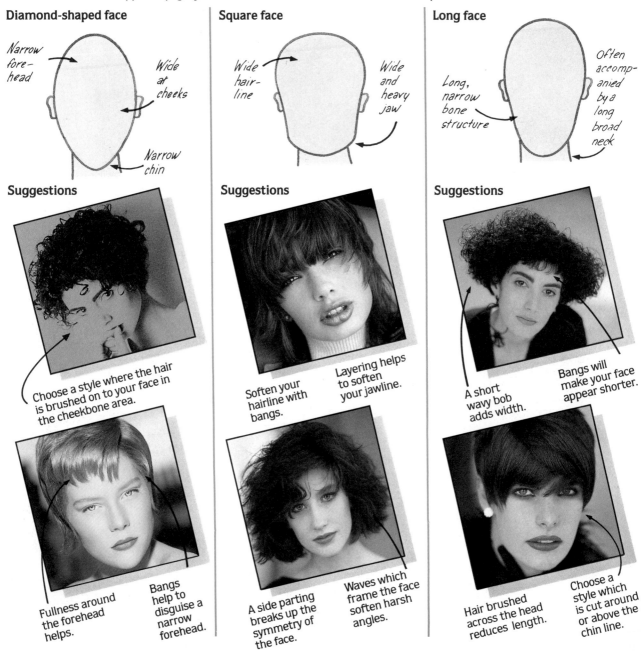

Diamond-shaped face

Narrow forehead

Wide at cheeks

Narrow chin

Suggestions

Choose a style where the hair is brushed on to your face in the cheekbone area.

Fullness around the forehead helps.

Bangs help to disguise a narrow forehead.

Square face

Wide hairline

Wide and heavy jaw

Suggestions

Soften your hairline with bangs.

Layering helps to soften your jawline.

A side parting breaks up the symmetry of the face.

Waves which frame the face soften harsh angles.

Long face

Long, narrow bone structure

Often accompanied by a long broad neck

Suggestions

A short wavy bob adds width.

Bangs will make your face appear shorter.

Hair brushed across the head reduces length.

Choose a style which is cut around or above the chin line.

What shape is your face?

To find out what shape your face is, measure it with a ruler, following the steps on the right. Write each measurement down and compare the results with the table provided.

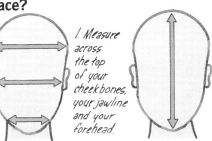

1. Measure across the top of your cheekbones, your jawline and your forehead.

2. Then measure from your hairline to your chin.

Oval	Length equal to one and a half times width.
Round	Almost as wide as it is long.
Long	Longer than it is wide.
Heart	Narrow at jawline, wide at forehead and cheekbones.
Square	Forehead, jawline and cheekbones almost equal in width.
Diamond	Wide cheeks, narrow forehead and jawline.

Heart-shaped face

Wide fore-head

Wide at cheeks

Narrow chin

Round face

Wide hair-line

Fullness at and below the cheekbones

Neck often seems short

Oval face

Neither too wide or too long

Jawline in proportion to forehead

Suggestions

Avoid fullness near the cheeks.

Short cuts with fullness at the crown work well.

Bangs give balance.

A bob adds fullness around the jaw but lies flat against the cheeks.

Suggestions

Choose layered bangs rather than ones which are straight and heavy.

Short styles which give height work best.

Keep the sides of your hair short.

Use curls to create height, keeping the sides of your hair short.

Suggestions

Most styles flatter an oval face.

This style emphasizes the cheekbones.

You may be able to carry off an outrageous style, such as this one.

The varying angles and colors give the style great impact.

Making the most of yourself

Most of us have an attractive feature which we would like to emphasize. Below you can find out how, by choosing the right style, you can make that feature a focal point.

Below you can found out how, with clever cutting and hairstyling, you can play down less appealing prominent features.

Eyes. Choose a style where the hair is swept away from your forehead, as shown above.

Jawline. Choose a style that follows the line of your jaw. Fullness at the back will also emphasize your jawline.

Lips. A style where the hair is brushed on to your face will help to make your lips a focal point.

Cheekbones. Choose a style that follows the line of your cheekbones, as shown above.

Close-set eyes. A style where the hair is brushed on to your face around the eyes will reduce the area either side.

Short neck. A short, cropped style will make a short neck appear longer. Alternatively long hair worn up will have the same effect.

High forehead. A good way to disguise a high forehead is by choosing a style with sleek, straight bangs.

Deep-set eyes. Your eyes will look larger if you brush your hair up and away from your forehead in a style that is full around the temples.

Long neck. Wear your hair long to help to create the illusion of a shorter neck. If possible choose a curly style which will also add fullness.

Double chin. Keep the hair around your face above chin level to draw the eyes upwards. The back may be grown longer. A bob would be ideal.

Wearing glasses

If you wear glasses, make sure you take them to the hairdresser's with you. Then you can discuss with the hairdresser what style would complement your frames as well as your face as a whole.

If you wear your glasses all the time, then the hairdresser should ask you to put them on at different stages during your re-style. This ensures that the cut is not distorted when you wear your glasses.

Shorter styles that lie well above the ears allow your glasses to fit correctly.

Choose a style that lies well above or falls well below your ears. Haircuts in between tend to get caught underneath the glasses frames, or stick out at strange angles. It is also a good idea to avoid styles that have long bangs or that are brushed forward on to your face as these will get in the way of your glasses. If you have blond hair, delicate frames will probably suit you best. Bolder frames look good with darker hair.

Lifestyle

Your lifestyle is another important consideration when choosing a new hairstyle. However much you like a particular style, it is no use if it causes you practical problems. Below are some things you should consider.

Are you always rushing to get ready for school or work? If so, choose a cut which is quick and easy to style.

Do you play a lot of sport? If so, choose a short style, or one which can easily be tied back.

Do you swim regularly? If so, choose a style which does not rely on blow drying to stay in shape.

Do you study or have a desk job? If so, avoid long bangs that will flop forward on to your face.

Cost

Maintaining a hairstyle can be expensive. Short, geometric hairstyles in particular need frequent visits to the hairdresser to keep them in shape. Dyed hair can look unattractive if the roots are not regularly re-touched and a perm which is growing out can look unkempt. It is therefore important to be realistic about what you can afford to spend after the initial expense of a new hairstyle.

On the right are some points to bear in mind.

★ To keep your style in shape and your hair in good condition, you should have a trim every six weeks.

★ If you have a long, simple style, you may need to have it trimmed only every eight weeks, as long as it is in good condition.

★ A permanent all-over color will need to be re-touched every four weeks as by this time your re-growth will be about 1.3cm long and very noticeable.

★ Permanent highlights or lowlights can be re-touched when you feel it necessary as the re-growth is not as noticeable as that of an all-over color.

★ Re-perming your hair as it starts to grow out can be damaging. However, you will still need to have it trimmed regularly.

★ Bargain haircuts may not be the good value that they seem as you could get a poor style which needs reshaping.

Choosing a hairdresser

Once you have an idea of the kind of hairstyle you would like, you need to find a hairdresser you trust. Start with the salon. If it is within your price range and you like the look of the decor and the staff, you will probably be in tune with the stylist who cuts your hair. Below are some suggestions for things to consider when choosing a salon.

What to look for in a salon

The outside: you can tell quite a lot about a salon without going inside. Look at the style of the shop front, the name of the salon and the reception area. If they appeal, then there is a good chance that this is the right salon for you. There should also be a price list displayed. Check what things cost and whether you can afford a senior stylist.

Look for modern equipment such as blowdryers, mousses and large combs. Avoid salons that are cluttered with rollers, hairsprays and hooded dryers.

Barbicide jars show that the salon is careful about hygiene.

Photographs on the walls may give you ideas for a new style.

Shiny basins and well-swept floors are signs of a clean, well kept salon.

For a first appointment, you are usually booked in with any stylist who has a suitable vacancy. It is a good idea to ask for a consultation first. This gives you a chance to meet them and discuss possible styles. On the opposite page you can find out how to get the most out of a consultation, as well as some tips to bear in mind when you visit the salon.

The inside: a good salon will be clean, friendly and efficient. The receptionist should be attentive and helpful. Do not be rushed into making an appointment. Ask for a consultation (see right) and have a good look around. If you don't like the look of things, do not be afraid to leave. You are unlikely to get what you want in a salon which makes you feel uncomfortable or intimidated.

A range of shampoos and conditioners for sale is all part of a good professional service.

Decor should be simple, bright and well-lit.

Many salons play background music. This can be a good clue to the tastes of the staff.

Schools, training evenings and academies.

These provide an alternative, if you can't afford the prices in a top salon. In a school or at a training session*, your hair is cut and styled by a trainee, under the close supervision of an experienced tutor. Students learn different techniques on different days, so check the timetable before you go along. Provided you go at the right time, you can expect to have nearly as much choice in the style you have as you would get from a qualified stylist.

In an academy, your hair is styled by a qualified hairdresser who is learning advanced techniques. A stylist at this level usually wants to experiment more than a novice. As you are getting expert attention, the stylist will expect to have more influence over your choice of style, than if you were paying the full salon rate.

* These are usually held in salons.

Prices

Before booking an appointment check the salon's prices. A price list should be clearly displayed in reception.

★ Find out whether you pay more for a senior stylist. If you only want a trim, choose a junior stylist.

★ Look out for special offers, many salons have discounts on certain days, or concessions for people under 16.

★ See if there are any extras, such as a charge for conditioner.

★ Look out for coupons in magazines advertising discounts.

★ It is worth investigating salons that hand out leaflets in the street advertising special prices.

★ Ask if the salon has a school. Modelling for students can be a cheap way of having a re-style.

Consultations

Any reputable salon will give you a free consultation, if you ask for it. This is a chance to discuss with a stylist what you would like done, without committing yourself to an appointment.

It is good to have a vague idea of a style you would like, such as whether you want it long or short, straight or curly. Keep an open mind, though. Let the stylist feel your hair and assess its natural tendencies. Talk to him about yourself and your lifestyle; tell him what you like about yourself and what you would like to play down. That way you can choose a style which really suits you in the light of expert advice.

Your appointment

When you arrive for your appointment, you will be given a gown to protect your clothes. Then you will be seated in front of a mirror and the stylist will talk to you about what you want done (you may have changed your mind since the consultation).

Next your hair will be shampooed. This takes place in the washing area of the salon and is usually done by a junior. You will then be returned to the cutting chair, where your hair will be cut and styled. If you are having your hair colored or permed, you may have to move to another area of the salon for this stage. The hairdresser will show you the finished style from every angle using a back-mirror (see page 25).

Finally the stylist will brush down your clothes and accompany you back to the reception area to pay your bill.

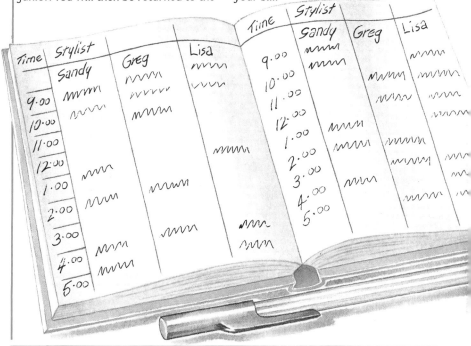

Dos and don'ts

★ Do ask for any tips and hints on styling your hair, so that you know how to maintain your new style.

★ Do tell the stylist what you really think of the finished style. It is not too late for minor adjustments if you are not completely happy with it.

★ Don't feel obliged to have extras such as conditioner, if you don't feel it is necessary.

★ Don't be afraid to tell the staff what's on your mind. For example, if the water is too hot or cold, when you are being shampooed, or if the stylist is cutting off too much hair.

★ Don't feel you have to leave a tip. If you are pleased with your new style and the service you received, you may want to give the hairdresser something to show your appreciation – it's for you to decide.

How often should you go?

When you have found a hairdresser you like, it is important to go back every six to eight weeks, for a trim. This will keep split ends at bay and your chosen hairstyle looking its best. Ask for your new stylist by name when you book the next appointment.

Hair care routine

Clean, well-groomed hair can make all the difference to the way you feel about yourself. Over time you may have picked up bad habits, such as using too much shampoo or not rinsing your hair adequately. By following the routine outlined on these two pages you will not only notice a marked improvement in your hair's condition but discover that taking extra time over your hair care can be relaxing and fun. All the equipment you need for your new routine is shown on the right.

Conditioner*. This smooths down the hair cuticle (see page 5), so that the hair is less likely to tangle and has a sheen when dry. Conditioners are available as light rinses or as rich oil or cream-based balsams.

Shampoo*. This removes dirt and grease from your hair. Wash your hair as often as you like using a shampoo formulated for your particular hair type (see opposite).

Hairdryer. There is more information on the type of dryer you should look for on page 45.

Shower. This provides constant clean water in which to flush away the dirt and grease in your hair. If you do not have a shower, use running tap water or a cup. Never rinse your hair in bath water as it is dirty and contains bits of flaking skin and harmful soap residue.

Wide-toothed comb. This is good for general use. A nylon comb with rounded ends is best. Metal or nylon combs with sharp teeth will tear your hair and are best avoided.

Towel

Styling brush. You can style hair with your fingers (see pages 30 and 31), but many people prefer to use a brush. Choose one with natural or synthetic bristles and rounded ends. To check the bristles, press them into your palm. If they hurt they are too sharp.

Shampooing and conditioning

Brush your hair to loosen any dirt and dead skin cells. Now wet your hair with luke-warm water. Pour a little shampoo into the palm of your hand. Dilute it slightly with water and rub your palms together to work up a lather.

Massage the shampoo into your hair with your fingertips, starting at your scalp and working right down to the ends. Now rinse it with luke-warm water until the water runs clear. Repeat if your hair is very dirty.

Pat your hair with a towel to soak up most of the moisture.** Gently massage a small amount of conditioner into your hair. Then comb it through, starting with the ends and working back gradually towards the roots.

Leave the conditioner on your hair for the time recommended on the bottle, then rinse it thoroughly in luke-warm water. Finally, rinse it for about 10 seconds in cold water. This will make your hair shinier.

* There is more information about the various shampoos and conditioners available on pages 42-43.
** If applied to soaking wet hair, the conditioner will be too dilute.

Blow drying

Pat your hair gently with a towel. Sit in front of a mirror which is close to a power point so that you can move the dryer around freely.

Divide your hair into sections. Dry the lower layers first, clipping the rest out of the way. Dry the back first, then the sides and top. Finish with the front and bangs.

Hold your dryer at least 10cm away from your hair. Put it on to a low setting and move gently back and forth until the section is dry.

As you dry your hair, lift it up. This gives it extra body and speeds up the drying process. Allow the hair to cool before removing the brush.

Brushing and combing

Brushing or combing your hair too often will damage it, so try not to do it more than two or three times a day.

Your hair is particularly vulnerable when it is wet, so always use a wide-toothed comb and treat it gently.

◀ Remove any tangles with a wide-toothed comb. Gently ease them free working through small sections of hair. Start at the ends and move up towards the roots. Hold your hair firmly to avoid pulling on the scalp.

Brush your hair starting at your scalp and moving towards the ends. Then bend forwards and brush the hair down from the nape of your neck. Finally, smooth your hair back in place with your hands. ▶

Type	Shampoo	Conditioner	Tips
Greasy	Mild shampoo formulated for greasy hair. These contain little, or no oil.	Light conditioning rinse (avoid oil-based or creamy conditioners). Apply to ends only.	Wash in luke-warm water and brush as little as possible. Use a natural bristle brush (this helps to absorb oil). Between washes, cleanse scalp with an astringent (see page 7).
Dry	Oil-enriched shampoo formulated for dry hair.	Use a cream or balsam conditioner after every wash.	If possible let hair dry naturally and avoid heated styling appliances. Use a conditioning oil treatment once a week. These can be bought or made-up at home (see page 6).
Combination	Very mild shampoo.	Oil-based conditioner. Apply to the ends of the hair only.	Use an astringent between washes (see page 7). Choose a style which can be left to dry naturally, rather than using heated appliances.
Normal	Mild shampoo.	Light conditioning rinse (not a cream conditioner) after every wash.	At the first sign of damage, treat with a single conditioning oil treatment (see page 6).

Special effects

Whether your hair is long or short, it is still possible to give it a totally different look and texture – be it for a party, on vacation or just for a change. The styling products and accessories shown here will give you some ideas. On page 44 you can find out about each individual product in more detail.

Mousse

Mousse adds body and texture to all hair types and is especially effective on styles that are scrunch dried (see page 31). You can buy regular or firm hold. Apply it to the roots of damp hair with your fingertips, then smooth it evenly through your hair with the palms of your hands.

Gel

Gel can be used to make shorter styles look spiky, or to keep a style in place to add body. Wet-look gel has a glossy finish. Apply gel to the roots of towel-dried or dry hair with your fingertips and then smooth it through with the palms of your hands.

Glaze

Glaze is stronger than gel and sets hard on your hair. It is particularly effective for slicking back curly or layered hair. Smooth it through towel-dried hair with the palms of your hands. Do not apply it to the roots of your hair.

Creams and greases

Creams and greases can give hair a healthy sheen or create a slicked-back wet look depending on how much you apply. Smooth it through wet or dry hair with the palms of your hands.

Finishing spray

Finishing spray coats the finished style in a fine mist of oil so that it looks healthy and shiny. It is especially effective on sleek, one-length styles and slicked-back hair. It can also be used to highlight different colors in hair.

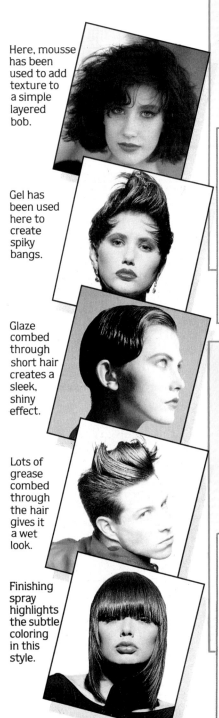

Here, mousse has been used to add texture to a simple layered bob.

Gel has been used here to create spiky bangs.

Glaze combed through short hair creates a sleek, shiny effect.

Lots of grease combed through the hair gives it a wet look.

Finishing spray highlights the subtle coloring in this style.

Accessories

Accessories such as ribbons, slides and combs are useful for keeping hair out of your way. They can also add variety to your hairstyle and allow you to color co-ordinate your clothes and hair.

When looking for new accessories, make sure that items such as slides and combs are strong enough to hold your hair in place and that they do not have sharp teeth or edges which might tear it. Choose colors which complement your clothes and stand out well against your hair color.

For a special occasion, colored chopsticks pushed through a top-knot give an oriental look.

Instant color

If you want a quick change of color for a party or a disco, try an instant spray-on hair color. This is a type of lacquer which coats the hair shaft with color. Sprays are available in a variety of vivid color and some even contain glitter or produce a metallic sheen on your hair. Instant colorants can either be washed or brushed out of your hair.

Here the hair has been sprayed several different colors.

Hair extensions

Hair extensions are made of fine strands of nylon which are melted around your natural hair. They are available in almost any color, texture or length. Hair extensions must be attached by a professional hairdresser. It is difficult and risky to attempt it yourself. Extensions last for up to four months (after this, the bond will begin to loosen) and are washed in the same way as normal hair. You can remove them by twisting the braid and gently snapping the seal.

The hair extension is placed on the parting of a small tress and the hair criss-crossed over the extension.

The real hair and the hair extension are then tightly plaited together and painted with a bonding solution.

A heated clamp melts the solution, sealing the extension around the hair. This is known as heat sealing.

Here, an intricate pattern has been painted onto the hair extensions.

Wigs and hair pieces

Synthetic wigs and hair pieces can be fun to wear and need not be too expensive. Some look and feel like real hair (these are the most expensive kind), others are brightly colored and are meant to look false (these can be bought very cheaply). Either type quickly and easily transforms your looks and needs minimal care. Before putting on a wig, pin your own hair into flat curls. Pull on the wig from the front holding it firmly at your forehead.

Hair pieces can either be plaited into your hair or attached with grips.

Disguise unkempt hair which is in poor condition with a wig.

Use hair pieces to add body or length.

Wigs and hair pieces should be brushed and shampooed regularly. Clean them in cool water and leave them to drip-dry. They automatically revert to their original shape when they are dry.

To store wigs and hair pieces, wrap them in tissue paper and put in a box in a cool place. Alternatively, wigs can be turned inside out and hung on a doorknob or on a special wig block.

Braiding

Braiding is a traditional technique used to style Afro hair. The hair is divided into lots of tiny little plaits which can be decorated with ribbons or beads and arranged in various styles.

Braided hair can be left in place for up to two months*. To keep it clean use a hand shower and direct the water along the partings so that the shampoo washes through the hair. Rosemary or almond oil, rubbed gently into your scalp, will help keep it healthy.

Braiding. Divide long hair into small square sections and braid them tightly. Seal the ends with wax or tie them with cotton.

Cornrowing. Part short hair into long thin rows. Braid each row tightly against the head, weaving wisps of hair into the braid to give a neat finish.

Wrapping. Wind special cotton thread tightly around sections of hair. You can then arrange the strands into intricate patterns on the head.

Do not braid or wrap your hair for longer than this. It strains the scalp and can cause hair loss.

Nostalgic hairstyles

This century, variety in women's hairstyles has increased enormously. This is because of changing attitudes (which have made short hair acceptable for women) and the development of new styling techniques, such as perming.

Innovations in men's hairdressing have been slower to develop. However, since the 1950s, men have also enjoyed a wider choice of styles.

Here you can see the hairstyles for which each decade, from the 1920s to the 1980s, is best remembered.

1920s

In the 1920s, women began to wear their hair short for the first time. This complemented a fashion for simple, uninhibiting clothes and shorter skirts. A silent film star called Louise Brooks popularised the bob (see page 26).

Men's hairstyles of the 1920s were short and smart. Oil was often used to slick the hair back and make it glossy.

Louise Brooks popularised the bob.

Rudolph Valentino, a famous screen idol, wore a typical 1920s hair style.

1950s

Men's and women's hairstyles changed dramatically in the 1950s.

Young men started to evolve distinctive styles of their own, based on teen idols such as Elvis Presley, James Dean and Buddy Holly. Hair was worn much longer (sometimes collar-length). It was slicked back, as before, but often with a huge, exaggerated quiff at the front.

Elvis Presley's hairstyle was his trademark.

Audrey Hepburn in the film 'Breakfast at Tiffany's'

It was still fashionable for women to wear their hair up. Teenage girls wore pony tails. Older women favoured back-combing which involved combing the hair upwards, then teasing it back towards the roots to give body. The hair could then be piled high on the head and sculpted into outlandish shapes. The finished style would be kept in place using hairspray.

1970s

In the early 70s, the graduated cut (see pages 28-29) and the shaggy perm made hair care easier than ever before as both looks required minimal styling. The feather cut was popular with men and women alike. It was short on top, with long, wispy strands of hair framing the face. Rock star David Bowie and film star Jane Fonda both wore versions of the feather cut.

Casual, wash and wear styles were a feature of the 1970s.

This Mohican hairstyle was popular with 70s punks.

In the mid 70s, punk rock music inspired a new fashion cult in which hair played a large part.

Punks rejected conventional fashion, wearing clothes which were often deliberately ripped or defaced with graffiti. They dyed their hair bright colors, such as green or orange, and used sprays or gels to sculpt it into threatening spiky styles.

1930s

In the 1930s, film stars such as Jean Harlow inspired women to dye their hair and wear it longer.

1940s

Long hair continued to be popular for women in the 1940s. Now however, it was more often worn up or tied back, with rolls or waves to give fullness at the front. A new and better perming method made curly hair more popular than ever.

The only difference between men's hairstyles of the 1940s and those of the 1920s was that side, partings became the fashion.

Joan Crawford wearing a typical 1940s hair style.

Clark Gable. Men's hair cuts had not changed much since the 1920s.

1960s

The 60s was a time of great variety. Informal looks which were easy to care for matched the relaxed attitudes of the decade. Vidal Sassoon revived the bob, but gave it a distinctive modern look by using revolutionary cutting and blow drying techniques. This made it an emblem of the times.

During the late 60s, long hair was fashionable for both sexes.

The 1960s version of the bob.

Afro styles or long hair characterized the hippy look.

The Beatles influenced men's hair styles.

1980s

The casual, sporty hairstyles of the early 80s gave way, by the middle of the decade, to several more stylised looks. These often featured short, rounded bangs and geometric lines. Although they appeared very formal, such styles did not actually require much attention to keep in shape. The 20s-style crop made a come-back in the 80s (this time dyed blonde).

A bleached crop

The 50s flat-top was revived for men.

Men's hairstyles got shorter and shorter until the late 80s. Towards the middle of the decade, there was a trend for cropped styles with a small plait at the nape. Later, a flat-top style, reminiscent of the 1950s took over from this. Long hair for men was also revived, but the 80s version was sleek and well-groomed, unlike the unkempt styles of the 60s.

Becoming a hairdresser

Hairdressing is a popular and exciting career which requires a wide variety of skills and personal attributes, from physical fitness to artistic judgement. Hairdressing training is undergoing important changes which will result in more possibilities for travel and variety of work than ever before, as the skills needed to do the job become standardized internationally. Here you can find out about the personal qualities you need to enter the profession, your promotion prospects and where hairdressing might lead you.

What does it take to be a hairdresser?

Below you can find out what kind of person makes a good hairdresser. It is worth considering not only whether you are right for the job, but also whether it is right for you.

Don't be put off if you are weak in some areas; many of the skills come with training. The first requirement is enthusiasm and an awareness of what hairdressing involves.

Physical qualities

Hairdressers are on their feet most of the day, and some of the styling techniques are demanding physically, so you will need to be fit.

Trainees keep the salon clean and tidy. This can be tiring.

Do not go into hairdressing if you suffer from skin disorders, such as eczema. Constantly getting your hands wet and handling strong chemicals may make your condition worse.

Some hairdressing techniques require good co-ordination.

Most of the tasks involved in cutting hair require manual dexterity (the ability to handle tools efficiently). This comes with practice, but it helps if you have good co-ordination.

Personal attributes

You will need to be patient and reasonably outgoing. Learning to communicate well and deal with people sympathetically comes with practice. It helps if you are naturally a sociable person and have an easy-going temperament.

A client who is disappointed with her new hairstyle needs to be treated with tact.

As well as requiring technical skills, hairdressing is also a creative and artistic job. If you are attracted by it, then you probably have some interest in fashion and beauty. Try to cultivate this and develop an eye for color and a sense of shape, symmetry and proportion.

Qualifications

You need a good basic education to be a hairdresser. You should be literate (able to read and write well) and numerate (able to do basic math). These skills are particularly important if your ambition is to become a salon manager. A manager needs to be able to communicate well (verbally and on paper) and to understand basic accounting and stock control methods.

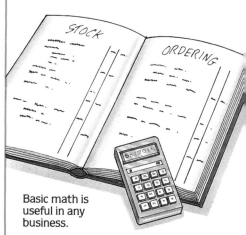

Basic math is useful in any business.

Any further qualifications you may have need not be wasted in hairdressing. For example, languages are useful if you want to work abroad (see opposite) and history could help you to get a job in film or television (see page 40).

Training as a hairdresser

Training schemes vary in format and length from country to country:

UK and Europe*

Training is currently being standardized so that each country's requirements of a newly qualified hairdresser are the same. This means that hairdressers will be able to move freely between countries and their skills will be recognized throughout the continent. On page 47 you can find out where to write for further information on training in the UK.

USA

In the USA you are expected to have a basic qualification in cosmetology (the science of skin and hair) before you can train as a hairdresser. On page 47, there is an address you can write to for details of hairdressing courses in the USA.

Advanced training

Once you are working as a hairdresser more advanced training is available which will give you the additional skills you need to climb the promotional ladder (see right). You may also have the opportunity to specialize in a particular area, or to learn management skills.

Competitions

Qualified hairdressers sometimes enter competitions. These can be run by companies which manufacture hairdressing products or alternatively, organized between several salons in one chain.

Competitions help to keep stylists in touch with new developments and provide them with an opportunity to experiment creatively.

Winning a competition can help a stylist's reputation and employment prospects.

Salons benefit from the publicity which competitions attract.

Promotion prospects

The ladder on the right represents the promotion route which exists in most salons. Once qualified, a hairdresser can decide whether to stay in the salon and progress up the ladder (following the blue arrows) or whether to move sideways, into a different area of the industry (following the pink arrows).

Specialize in one area and become advisor to large organization.

Teach in a hairdressing school.

Become a ship's hairdresser or work abroad.

Move into films, theatre or television.

School or other career

Salon manager. May be senior stylist. Recruits and supervises staff. Handles staff problems. Deals with salon finance, public relations and publicity. Sometimes acts as creative director, developing the salon's image and 'market profile'.

Senior stylist. Cuts, barbers, perms and colors hair to a very high professional standard. Develops creative talents. May start to specialize in one area, such as coloring or perming.

Stylist. Cuts, barbers, perms and colors hair to a high professional standard. May do advanced hairdressing courses and enter competitions.

Junior stylist (or first year operator). Cuts, barbers, perms and colors hair to a professional standard without supervision.

Trainee. Shampoos hair. Does roller setting, pin curling, finger waving. Learns science of skin and hair and salon etiquette. Learns basic cutting, barbering, coloring and perming. Cleans salon. Helps stylists.

Become an executive in a large hairdressing company or manage own chain of salons.

Work for the fashion and advertising businesses (styling hair for catwalk shows or photography sessions) as well as in a salon.

Demonstrate hairstyling products (see page 40-41).

Equipment

As a trainee hairdresser, you will be learning the practice as well as the theory of hairdressing.

On these two pages you can find out about all the equipment you will be using.

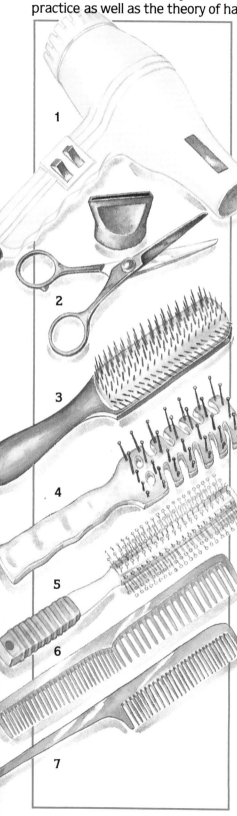

Hairdresser's own equipment

1. Hairdryer. Choose a lightweight, powerful dryer with several different temperature settings.

2. Scissors. These are a hairdresser's most important tool and it is well worth spending the money to buy a really good pair. Your employer or course tutor should be able to advise you on where to buy them from. Look for a pair with short blades (about 10-11cm long) as these will give you maximum control. Have your scissors sharpened regularly, as blunt blades create an uneven cutting line.

3. Styling brush. For general styling, choose a brush with rounded nylon bristles set into a flexible rubber pad. This type of brush is very hygienic, as it can be taken apart for cleaning.

4. Vent brush. When styling curly hair, you will need a brush with rounded nylon bristles, set into a flat, vented base.

5. Radial brush. Good for blow-drying hair in a curly style.

6. Wide-toothed comb. Choose a comb made of plastic or hardened rubber. The teeth should have rounded ends.

7. Tail comb. Useful for separating tresses when coloring or curling hair (using the tail). The teeth should have rounded ends and should be made of plastic or hardened rubber. The tail may be metal.

8. Spray mist. Useful for dampening sections of hair which may have started to dry during cutting.

9. Neckbrush. For removing tiny strands of hair from your client's neck and face.

10. Sectioning clips. For clipping hair out of your way while you work on a particular section.

11. Appointments diary. For writing down your own daily schedule.

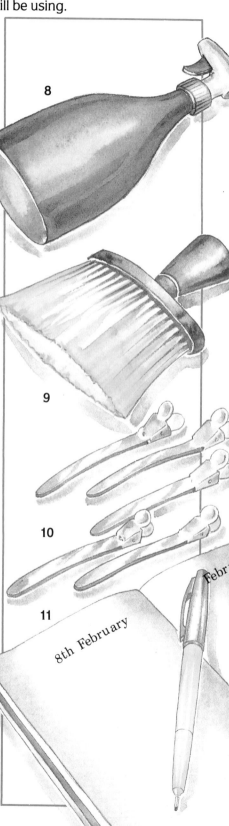

Salon equipment

All salons have the following basic equipment:

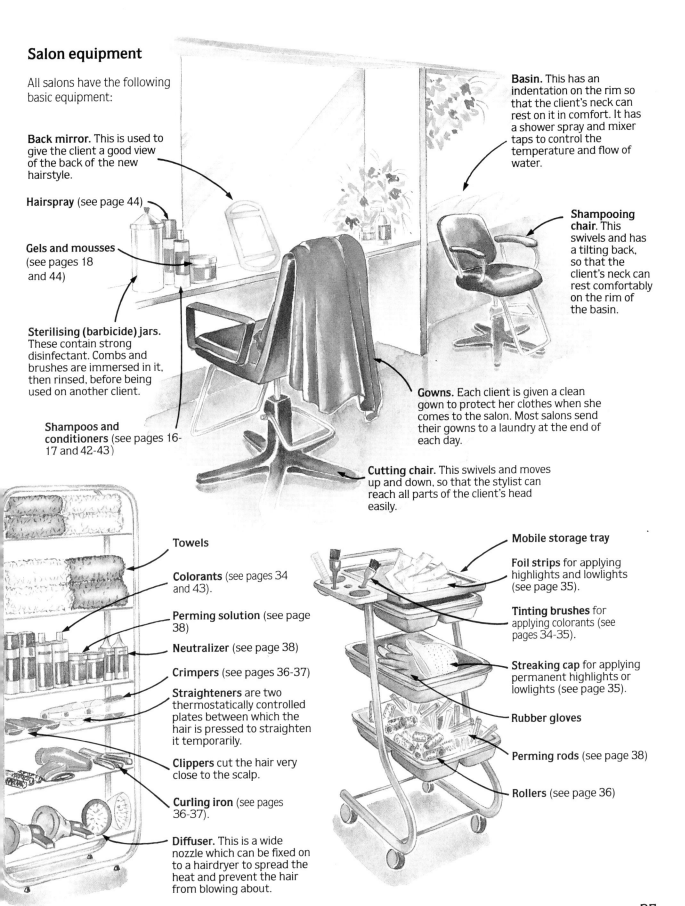

Back mirror. This is used to give the client a good view of the back of the new hairstyle.

Hairspray (see page 44)

Gels and mousses (see pages 18 and 44)

Sterilising (barbicide) jars. These contain strong disinfectant. Combs and brushes are immersed in it, then rinsed, before being used on another client.

Shampoos and conditioners (see pages 16-17 and 42-43)

Basin. This has an indentation on the rim so that the client's neck can rest on it in comfort. It has a shower spray and mixer taps to control the temperature and flow of water.

Shampooing chair. This swivels and has a tilting back, so that the client's neck can rest comfortably on the rim of the basin.

Gowns. Each client is given a clean gown to protect her clothes when she comes to the salon. Most salons send their gowns to a laundry at the end of each day.

Cutting chair. This swivels and moves up and down, so that the stylist can reach all parts of the client's head easily.

Towels

Colorants (see pages 34 and 43).

Perming solution (see page 38)

Neutralizer (see page 38)

Crimpers (see pages 36-37)

Straighteners are two thermostatically controlled plates between which the hair is pressed to straighten it temporarily.

Clippers cut the hair very close to the scalp.

Curling iron (see pages 36-37).

Diffuser. This is a wide nozzle which can be fixed on to a hairdryer to spread the heat and prevent the hair from blowing about.

Mobile storage tray

Foil strips for applying highlights and lowlights (see page 35).

Tinting brushes for applying colorants (see pages 34-35).

Streaking cap for applying permanent highlights or lowlights (see page 35).

Rubber gloves

Perming rods (see page 38)

Rollers (see page 36)

Professional cutting methods

Despite the apparent abundance of highly individual styles, they all evolved from one of three basic cuts – the bob, the graduated cut or the layered look.

Over the next eight pages you can find out how the professionals are taught these basic cuts and how, with the aid of new techniques and versatile styling products, the looks can be adapted to create a wider variety of styles than ever before.

All the cutting techniques illustrated here should be carried out under the supervision of a qualified instructor.

The rules of cutting

The secret of successful hairstyling is understanding your client's hair. Below are some basic rules. You can find out about the equipment you will need on pages 24-25.

1. Always cut hair wet, because:

★ Freshly washed hair is more hygienic to work with.
★ The hair is easier to control.
★ The client's head shape is clearly visible and the shape of the cut is more easily defined.
★ Washing the hair removes substances such as mousse or gel which affects the way it falls.

2. Use the natural shape of the head as a guideline when cutting.

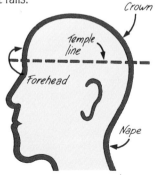

Here you can see the names given to the different parts of the head. These terms are used in the step-by-step cutting instructions which follow.

3. Consider the natural growth of the hair.

Hair grows from a natural base on the crown. This should dictate the way in which it is cut as working against the natural growth will result in a bad style. Hair also has a natural parting and hairline. A style which attempts to create an artificial line will look odd and may be hard to manage.

4. Hold the hair firmly but without tension.

Pulling hair tightly distorts the cutting line. The hair will spring back to its natural position once it is released, creating an uneven line.

5. Compensate for the ears

When cutting a style which covers the ears, compensate for the fact that they will make the hair lift slightly.

The bob

In the early 1920s, the silent filmstar, Louise Brooks, created a sensation by wearing her hair in a stark, chic style which became known as the bob. The look was revived amid great publicity in the 1960s, when Vidal Sassoon styled a bangless version for the actress Nancy Kwan. Since then, the bob has been consistently popular in one form or another.

The bob is a one-length hairstyle. This means that if an imaginary line is drawn horizontally around the bottom of the hair, all the ends touch it. A banged bob is just a variation on the same theme. All one-length styles, whether long or short, are based on this cut.

Probably the most versatile of the basic cuts, the bob can be adapted to suit almost any hair type and face shape. The sleek, sculptured look is ideal for heavy, straight hair, while wavy hair will produce a softer style and curly hair a really dramatic effect.

Adapting the basic cut

This subtle wavy effect has been achieved by cutting the bob short at the back and then gradually lengthening it towards the front of the head. A soft pin curl perm* has then been applied, and the hair left to dry naturally. ▶

There is more about this and other types of perm on pages 38-39.

Cutting*

1. Part the hair at the back and clip one side out of the way. On the free side, comb the bottom layer of hair on to the neck as shown. Cut the layer to length (this is known as 'cutting in the base line').

2. Comb down another layer of hair and hold it firmly in place at the nape. Using the base line as a guide, cut it the same length as before. Repeat this procedure until the back section is completed.

3. Move around to the side of the head. Hold the bottom layer of hair away from the neck as shown. This compensates for the ear. Cut the hair so that it lines up with the base line at the back of the head.

4. Working up towards the top of the head, gradually release fine layers of hair and cut each one to the length of the base line. Now repeat steps three and four on the other half of the head.

Drying

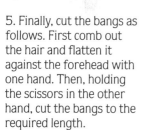

5. Finally, cut the bangs as follows. First comb out the hair and flatten it against the forehead with one hand. Then, holding the scissors in the other hand, cut the bangs to the required length.

6. Now hold the centre section of the bangs slightly away from the forehead, as shown. Cut it in a straight line. This creates a layered effect and gives the finished bangs a softer look.

1. Divide the hair into sections as for cutting. Hold the dryer about 10cm from the hair. Brush from underneath, directing the heat on to the brush as it moves from the roots to the ends of the hair.

2. Always point the hairdryer down towards the ends of the hair as you dry. Keep each section quite fine, and make sure that it is completely dry before moving on to the next one.

◄ These sides were cut by sliding the scissors along each tress**. This produces a mixture of lengths and reduces weight. It is known as 'slide cutting'.

The bangs have been cut a little further back than the temples, and curved slightly. When the hair is worn up, there is still a strong line around the face. ►

Here, the hair has been cut in a heavy square line. The front section was then twisted and slide cut (see left) to give an impression of ringlets. ◄

Remember, only cut hair under the supervision of a qualified instructor.
**A small section or lock of hair.*

27

The graduated cut

The graduated look combines a bold outline with a softer feathery effect. This look first became popular in the 1970s and is the basis for many of today's softer, shorter styles.

It is generally used to add body and movement to straight hair, but can also be successfully adapted to most hair types. The graduated cut suits most face shapes, although it is not recommended if you have a very heavy or wide jaw-line.

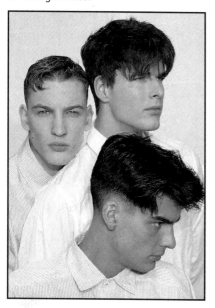

The most popular haircuts for men are based on the short graduated cut (as shown on the left) and the short layered cut (shown on pages 32-33). Long hair for men has been in fashion from time to time, particularly in the late 60s when the hippy look was popular.

Cutting*

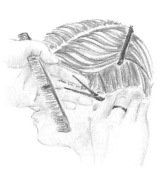

1. First comb the hair and let it fall into its natural parting. Now, taking this into account, cut the basic outline shape. This is called the base line, and dictates the length of the cut.

2. Comb down the bottom layer of hair on one side and clip the rest out of your way. To create a soft line, hold the hair away from the head and cut to the required length.

4. When you reach the layers of hair closest to the temple line, hold them downwards, much closer to the head as shown. This helps to create a much stronger line.

5. When you reach the final layer of hair, hold the hair out horizontally from the head and cut to length. This gives an even, rounded shape to the finished cut.

Drying

7. Cut the bangs last as it is easier to judge the final length when almost dry. Hold the bangs slightly forward and cut on a curve to create a heavy rounded effect.

1. To dry the hair, divide it into sections in the same way as you did for cutting. Using a styling brush and hairdryer, follow the same technique as for drying the bob (see page 27).

Remember, only cut hair under the supervision of a qualified instructor.

3. Separate the next layer of hair and cut it so that it falls just below the first one. Continue in this way until you reach the layer of hair which is nearest to the temple line.

6. Repeat this method on the other side. When you have completed both sides, graduate the back in the same way, to reduce the hair between the nape and crown.

2. If you want the finished look to be soft and feathery, use the brush to turn the hair outwards, rather than inwards. This gives a slight curve to the top sections of hair.

Adapting the basic cut

It is easy to transform the basic graduated cut into a glamorous look for evenings.

Here, mousse was applied to the roots, then the hair was directed upwards and backwards while being finger dried (see page 31).

You can find out more about mousse and other styling products on page 44. ▶

To achieve the effect shown here, naturally curly or wavy hair has been left to dry by itself.

Straight hair would need to be softly permed after it has been cut in a graduated style. The hair would then be left to dry naturally. ▶

This naturally curly graduated cut has been made more dramatic by clipping the hair very short at the back and sides.

First, the basic style was cut. Then clippers (see page 25) were used to cut the hair very close to the head. This technique is known as 'cropping'. ▶

Here, a deep base line has been cut to create a fuller, heavier graduated style. This is known as a 'rounded graduation'

The lower layers have been tinted a darker shade than the rest of the hair to give them added depth. The hair has then been styled using a generous amount of mousse to give it extra body. ▶

To produce the spiky effect shown here, scissors have been woven in and out of small sections of hair so that some sections are cut shorter than others. The shorter sections have been spaced as evenly as possible.

This technique is known as 'weave cutting'. The finished effect is one of added height and body. ▶

Layering short hair

The basic layered cut can be worn short or long, and for this reason, it is probably the most popular look in modern hairdressing.

Originally regarded as a cut for men, the short layered look was adopted by women in the early 1920s.

Shorter hairstyles and less restrictive clothing were popular at this time because women had worked outside the home during the First World War and this led to a new mood of emancipation and practicality afterwards. One of the most extreme cuts to emerge was the Eton crop (named after the famous English boy's school) for which the hair was cut very short around the ears.

The short layered cut is a style that is suited to all hair types and can be adapted to flatter almost all the basic face shapes.

Cutting*

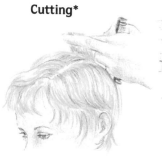

1. Starting at the top of the head, separate a section of hair from the crown, as shown. Comb the rest of the hair out of the way and clip if necessary.

2. Hold the hair horizontally, and pull it forward towards the front of the head. Cut the hair straight across. Repeat with each layer until you reach the bang area.

3. To check that you have cut the hair evenly, hold it lengthways, as shown. Trim off any uneven ends leaving the hair slightly longer near the crown.** This is 'cross-checking'.

4. Cut the back section starting at the crown and working down towards the nape. Take a layer of hair from the back of the crown and hold it vertically, as shown.

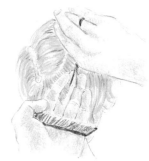

5. Pull the hair slightly away from the head and cut it with the scissors pointing towards the nape of the neck, rather than across the head. Repeat until all the hair is cut.

6. Now check that the back section is the correct length by holding the hair horizontally as shown, and trimming away any of the ends which are not aligned (cross-checking).

7. Cut the sides from the crown downwards in the same way as the back. Check that the layers are even by running the fingers up through the hair. Trim any uneven ends.

8. To cut the bangs, hold them out slightly from the forehead and cut so they fall in a soft line. Finally, trim the base line to the required length. This gives the cut its shape.

* Remember, only cut hair under the supervision of a qualified instructor.
** If the hair is too short near the crown it will stick up when dry.

Drying

The best way to style short layered hair is by running your fingers through it, or scrunching it (see right) until it dries. These techniques give the hair an attractive tousled look. Allowing hair to dry naturally is better for it. However, this is not always possible in the salon. You can speed up the technique shown here and still achieve a similar result by using a hairdryer on a low setting.

Finger drying: First towel dry the hair, leaving it slightly damp. Then massage through a generous amount of mousse (see page 44) to keep the style in place. Keeping your fingers straight, run each hand alternately through the hair, at the same time lifting it up from the roots to add body and movement to the finished style. ▶

Scrunch drying: Towel dry the hair until it is only slightly damp and add plenty of mousse. Arrange roughly the style you want. Then take handfuls of hair and scrunch them gently in your fist, using the palm of your hand to push the hair up from the scalp. As you scrunch the hair, gently massage it with your fingers to remove all the moisture. ◀

Adapting the basic cut

Here, the hair has been 'twist cut' in order to achieve a full, bouncy texture. This technique involves taking small sections of the hair and twisting them, before cutting. ▶

Color can then be added to make the look even more dramatic, as here.

To create this stunning effect, the hair has been cut in very short layers, then gel applied to the roots. The hair was then finger dried (see above). Finally, the tips of the hair were tinted a slightly darker color (there is more about coloring hair on pages 34-35). ▶

To produce soft, wispy bangs, small sections of hair have been cut every few millimetres, with the scissors pointing down towards the ends of the hair. This cutting technique is known as 'pointing'. ▶

To give a cut this unusual elongated shape, the hair has been left much longer at the crown than normal. This creates fullness. The short sides and back add to the impression of height. Gel has then been used to keep the hair in place. ▶

For this look, the layers on the top of the head have been left fairly long, and the back and sides cropped very short. This gives an impression of fullness which is complemented by the solid, rounded bangs. ▶

Here, a soft pin curl perm** has been applied to give variety of texture to a straight layered cut. This creates a very subtle soft wave through the top layer of hair. In addition, the model's bangs have been 'pointed' (see left). ▶

You can find out more about applying gel on page 18.
**There is information on perming on pages 38-39.*

Layering long hair

The long layered cut became popular in the early 1970s. It provided a whole new range of styles for people who preferred to wear their hair longer, and a softer alternative to the more severe short layered cut.

Long layered cuts have remained extremely popular in the 1980s as they flatter most face shapes, are easy to maintain and suit almost all hair types. The only things which restrict people from choosing them is having brittle hair or hair with a short life-span (see pages 4-5). Layering longer hair gives it extra body, while making it easier to style and quicker to dry.

The cutting technique used is similar to that for short hair (see pages 30-31), however the layers are left much longer and the cutting stages are reversed so that the basic outline is cut before layering begins, rather than afterwards.

Cutting*

1. Starting with the bangs, hold the hair out at a slight angle from the head, as shown. Carefully cut the hair to the required length, little by little.

2. Move around to the side. Again holding the hair out at a slight angle, cut it to length. This creates a soft outline when the hair dries. Repeat on the other side.

3. Hold the hair at the back of the head against the neck or back** of the client and cut it to length. This establishes the outline (base line) of the cut.

4. To layer the hair, start with the area in front of the crown. Comb out a section of hair and hold it forwards. Cut the hair straight across.

5. Continue in the same way until all the hair in front of the crown is layered. Then move to the sides and layer them as you did the front section.

6. When you reach the crown, hold each layer of hair straight out to the side. This reduces the weight of the top layers. Cut as before.

7. Move around to the back of the head and layer the hair between the nape of the neck and the crown, using the the same method as described in stage 6.

8. Finally, check that the base line is even and cross-check the layers (see page 30) to make sure that there are no untidy ends visible.

*Remember, only cut hair under the supervision of a qualified instructor.
**This depends on the finished length required by the client.

Drying

The long layered cut should ideally be left to dry naturally. This gives it a natural look and is better for the hair. However, in a salon there will not be time to do this. The following steps show you how to achieve a similar effect using gel and a hairdryer.

When drying a client's hair, try to explain what you are doing so that they feel confident about styling their new cut at home.

Towel dry the hair, leaving it slightly damp. Then apply a generous amount of gel (see page 18) to the roots with your fingertips.

Blow dry the roots by lifting the hair with your fingers and directing the heat down into the hair (from at least 10cm away).

If possible, leave the ends of the hair to dry naturally as this will give it added body. It also creates an attractive tousled effect.

Adapting the basic cut

Here you can see how wet-look gel can be effective on long hair. Gel has been combed through the hair, which has then been formed into waves with the fingers. A few strands of hair have been loosened to ▶ soften the look.

Here, the bangs have been 'pointed' (see page 31) to give a wispy look. To emphasize the layers, the hair has been highlighted with two complementary colors. It has then been finger dried. ▶

This effect has been achieved on naturally curly hair by cutting the top layers short and leaving the sides and back layers longer. The hair has then been scrunch dried (see page 31). If the hair were straight, it would need to be permed on large rollers first. ▶

To produce this crinkly effect, the hair has been permed on pipe cleaners, and the ends left free. It has then been 'weave cut' (see page 29), and cropped short around the forehead. It has been dried using gel. ▶

Here, long, straight hair has been permed on rollers of different sizes to give it a variety of textures. It has then been left to dry naturally. To achieve a soft, romantic effect, the hair around the temples has then been swept away from the ▶ face and piled loosely on top of the head.

The basic long layered cut works well on naturally wavy hair. To emphasize the soft, feathery effect of the cut, subtle highlights have been added around the face. The hair has then been ▶ dried using the technique described at the top of the page.

Professional coloring methods

A change of hair color can give new life to a style you are bored with, and trying out different effects can be fun. However, hair colorants are potentially damaging, so it is advisable to have them applied by a professional hairdresser. If you do want to color your hair at home, use a colorant that does not alter your hair chemically (see below) and check with your hairdresser first.

Tools of the trade

Below are some of the tools used for coloring hair.

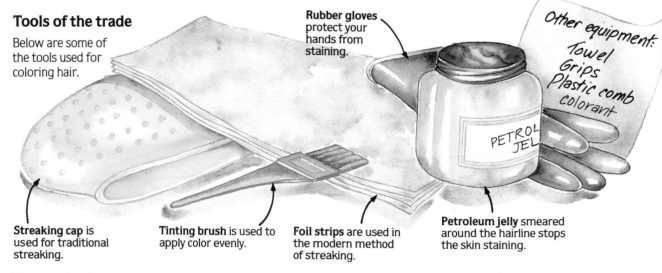

Rubber gloves protect your hands from staining.

Other equipment:
Towel
Grips
Plastic comb
colorant

PETROL JEL

Streaking cap is used for traditional streaking.

Tinting brush is used to apply color evenly.

Foil strips are used in the modern method of streaking.

Petroleum jelly smeared around the hairline stops the skin staining.

Types of colorant*

Colorants work by staining the hair shaft with color. The length of time a color lasts depends on how far it penetrates the hair shaft.

Temporary colorants coat the hair shaft with a thin layer of color which is removed by shampooing.** Apply them to damp hair in the form of a liquid or mousse, or on to styled hair if you are using gel, spray or paints.

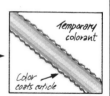

temporary colorant

Color coats cuticle

Semi-permanent colorants last longer than temporary colorants because they enter the cuticle. Apply them to clean hair in the form of a creamy shampoo or mousse.

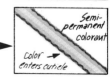

Semi-permanent colorant

Color enters cuticle

Permanent colorants (dyes) or bleaches (see page 43) penetrate deep into the cortex. When mixed with a chemical called hydrogen peroxide they actually change the pigment in the hair (see page 4). Apply them to dry hair.

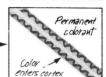

Permanent colorant

Color enters cortex

Metallic colorants are used on greying hair and are known as progressive dyes as the color develops after several applications. They contain lead or silver salts which slowly change color. Apply as a liquid on to dry hair.

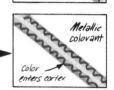

Metallic colorant

Color enters cortex

Vegetable colorants are available in two types. One type coats the cuticle and is applied as an infusion (see page 7). The other, henna for example, penetrates the cortex. Natural dyes fade, so must be applied regularly to maintain the color.

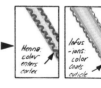

Henna: color enters cortex

Infus-ions: color coats cuticle

Testing colorants

The following tests should be done before coloring your hair, whether at a hairdresser's, or at home.

Strand test: to check that a color suits you, dip a few strands of your hair in the colorant. Leave for the recommended time and rinse clean.

Skin test: Dab a little colorant on the inside of your elbow. Leave for a few hours. If your arm itches or turns red, do not use the product.

Dos and don'ts when coloring at home

★ Do follow the manufacturer's instructions carefully.

★ Do a skin and strand test first.

★ Don't choose a red tint if you have a flushed or ruddy complexion.

★ Don't try bleaching naturally red hair as it will turn a brassy yellow.

★ Don't choose a dark shade if you have a fair complexion.

* There is more information on colorants on page 43.
** You may find that there are still traces of color after one wash.

Applying color

Below you can find out about two of the most popular methods of coloring.

Overall color

1. Divide the hair into quarters by creating two partings: one from the forehead to the nape of the neck and one across the centre of the head.

2. Apply the color to the ends of the hair and leave for 15 minutes. Then apply to the roots and leave for a further 15 minutes.

3. Rinse thoroughly. Shampoo and condition the hair and then style it as normal. The finished effect should be even color.

Foil highlights or lowlights*

1. Separate a section of hair. With a tail comb (see page 24) weave in out of the section picking up fine tresses of hair.

2. Place the foil under the tresses and use a tinting brush to paint on the colorant.

3. Fold the foil around the hair. Repeat with each section. Leave for the recommended time.

4. Remove the foil strips starting with the first section you did. Rinse thoroughly. Shampoo and condition as normal.

Alternative techniques

Batiking. Lighten the hair and apply petroleum jelly to the areas where no further color is wanted. Paint the exposed areas in three complementary colors. Now comb the hair lightly to blend the colors. The result is a subtle mixture of random colors.

Streaks. Dry hair is combed ▶ into its usual style, then a streaking cap pulled tightly on top. Small strands of hair are then pulled through the holes with a hook, and color applied to them. Once the color has taken effect, the cap is removed, and the hair is rinsed and shampooed thoroughly.

Slices. The hair is combed ▶ into its usual style, then separated into tresses. Each tress is then divided (or sliced) in half widthways, and color is applied to the half nearest the scalp. When the color has taken effect, the hair is rinsed thoroughly.

Flying colors. Color ▶ is applied to the tips of the hair with a brush and comb, then it is left for the recommended time. It is then rinsed, shampooed and styled as usual.

Applying henna

Henna is a natural dye which comes in powdered form. It colors and conditions your hair.

1. Mix the henna with warm water until it looks like mud. Comb it through clean, dry hair.

2. Wrap your hair in plastic wrap or an old towel. Then leave for up to an hour.**

3. Rinse out the henna, until the water runs clear. Finally, shampoo and style your hair as usual.

Highlights are lighter than your natural color and lowlights darker.
**Check the packet for guidelines on how long to leave the henna.*

Professional curling methods

The methods of curling shown here are all used by professional hairdressers. Unlike the cutting techniques shown on pages 26-33, curling can be done successfully at home. The right equipment helps (a selection of tools is shown below), and following the correct procedure is essential. With practice, you should be able to produce various looks – from corkscrew curls to soft waves.

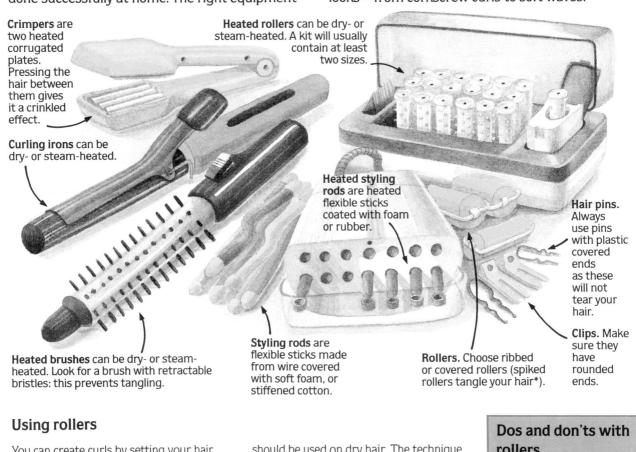

Crimpers are two heated corrugated plates. Pressing the hair between them gives it a crinkled effect.

Curling irons can be dry- or steam-heated.

Heated brushes can be dry- or steam-heated. Look for a brush with retractable bristles: this prevents tangling.

Heated rollers can be dry- or steam-heated. A kit will usually contain at least two sizes.

Heated styling rods are heated flexible sticks coated with foam or rubber.

Styling rods are flexible sticks made from wire covered with soft foam, or stiffened cotton.

Rollers. Choose ribbed or covered rollers (spiked rollers tangle your hair*).

Hair pins. Always use pins with plastic covered ends as these will not tear your hair.

Clips. Make sure they have rounded ends.

Using rollers

You can create curls by setting your hair on rollers. Cold rollers should be used on damp, towel-dried hair. Heated rollers should be used on dry hair. The technique is the same whether you use hot or cold rollers. You can see what to do below.

Starting at the front of your crown (see page 26), hold a small section of hair upwards. Wind it neatly around a roller, as shown. Then roll it down on to your head and secure it with a grip.

Repeat until the top of the head is done. For the back and sides, hold each section of hair slightly away from your head and wind the rollers towards your scalp from underneath. Secure as before.

Now leave your hair to dry. To test it, carefully unwind a roller from the thickest part of your hair. If the hair is dry, carefully remove the rest of the rollers and gently comb your hair through.

Dos and don'ts with rollers

★ Do tuck tissue paper around the ends of your hair if it is short or cut in a layered or graduated style. This makes the hair easier to roll and ensures that it lies flat giving a smooth finish.

★ Don't remove rollers before your hair is completely dry. If you do, your hair may go frizzy rather than curly.

★ Don't try to roll too much hair on to each roller or you will find that the roller falls out of your hair.

If you have spiked rollers don't throw them away; snip off the spikes and file the stumps smooth with an emery board.

Using styling rods

You can use styling rods to make ringlets, waves or curls. Use cold rods on towel-dried hair, or heated rods on clean, dry or slightly damp hair.

Take a small section of hair and lightly twist it between your thumb and forefinger along its full length.

Wind the tress around a styling rod, and secure the ends*. Repeat until you have curled all your hair.

Leave cold rods in overnight if possible. Heated rods can be removed after about 10-15 minutes.

Using curling irons and brushes

Curling irons and brushes create instant curls and waves on dry hair. They are quick and easy to use. The technique is the same for both brushes and curling irons.

Starting underneath, take a tress and clip the rest of the hair out of your way. Grip the end of the tress in the brush or iron.

Wind the tress around the brush or iron towards your scalp. Hold for a few seconds then release carefully.

Repeat until all the hair is curled. Leave the hair to cool before brushing through, otherwise it will go limp and flat.

Using crimpers

Crimpers produce a temporary crinkled effect on dry hair**. They are quick and easy to use and the result will last until your next shampoo.

Separate a lower layer of hair. Working from the roots down, grip sections of hair in the crimpers, hold, then release.

Separate the next layer of hair and crimp it in the same way. Work your way around your head, until all the hair is crinkly.

Allow your hair time to cool. Then run your fingers through it gently to merge the sections of hair together and give it body.

Occasional curling

If you only want to curl your hair once in a while, you need not buy expensive heated appliances. You can achieve a similar effect by using a radial brush (see page 24) and your hairdryer.

1. Wind a small section of hair tightly around a small radial brush.

2. Dry the section with a hairdryer.

3. Gently remove the brush without unwinding the curl, and secure it against your head with a grip.

4. Repeat until all your hair has been curled. Leave for half an hour.

5. Remove the grips and loosen the curls with your fingers.

Dos and don'ts with heated appliances

★ Do use a conditioner or styling mousse to protect your hair.

★ Do invest in steam-heated appliances if you often use rollers, curling irons or brushes, as these are unlikely to damage your hair.

★ Do make sure that you unplug them immediately after use.

★ Don't use them as part of your daily styling routine as they dry and damage your hair.

★ Don't leave them in your hair for longer than necessary, as you may scorch and damage your hair.

★ Don't use electrical appliances in the bathroom or near water.

* Different styling rods are secured in different ways. Check the packet for instructions.
** You can achieve a similar effect by plaiting your hair when wet and leaving it to dry overnight.

Professional perming methods

With modern perming techniques you can achieve a wide range of textures, from a light, bouncy wave to a mass of curls. The look of a perm depends on the size and pattern of perming rods used and on the style in which the hair is cut. Below you can see how a basic perm is done. On the opposite page there are some examples of effects that can be achieved by varying the technique.

Tools of the trade

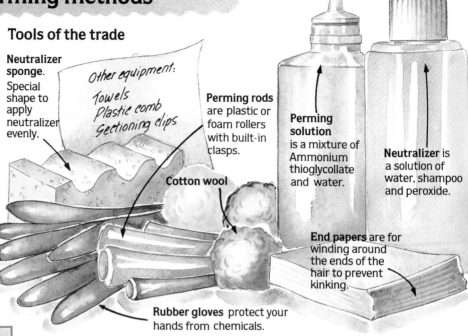

Neutralizer sponge. Special shape to apply neutralizer evenly.

Other equipment:
Towels
Plastic comb
Sectioning clips

Perming rods are plastic or foam rollers with built-in clasps.

Cotton wool

Perming solution is a mixture of Ammonium thioglycollate and water.

Neutralizer is a solution of water, shampoo and peroxide.

End papers are for winding around the ends of the hair to prevent kinking.

Rubber gloves protect your hands from chemicals.

How perming works

A perm breaks down the chemical bonds between the molecules in the hair shaft and then reconnects them in a different pattern.

Straight hair with molecules bonded in a fixed pattern.

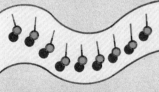

1. Hair is wound on to perming rods and perming solution is applied. It enters the cortex and breaks up the bonds between the molecules.

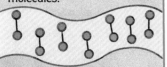

2. When neutralizer is added, the molecules reconnect, setting the hair in a curly pattern.

Perming technique*

1. Wash and towel-dry the hair. Comb out a small section of hair from the back of the crown and clip the rest out of your way. Fold a paper around the ends of the hair, as shown.

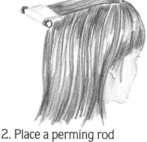

2. Place a perming rod underneath the paper and start to roll it up, gently but firmly, as shown. Continue until it rests comfortably on the scalp, then close the clasp.

3. Continue in the same way down the back of the head. Then move on to the sides and the front. Vary the size of the rods according to the texture you want to achieve.

4. Apply perming solution evenly all over the head, using the special applicator, leave on for the *exact* amount of time recommended by the manufacturer.

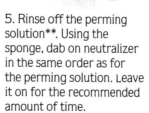

5. Rinse off the perming solution**. Using the sponge, dab on neutralizer in the same order as for the perming solution. Leave it on for the recommended amount of time.

6. Remove the rods and papers, then dab more neutralizer on the ends of the hair. Leave for a few more minutes. Rinse well. Finally, cut and style the hair as usual.

*Remember, you should only perm hair under the supervision of an experienced instructor.
** To shield the client's eyes, put a roll of cotton wool around her hairline while you do this.

Adapting the basic perm

Body perm. This is a soft, loose perm produced using large perming rods. This gives the hair height and volume, without making it very curly. A disadvantage of this perm is that it will start to drop out after seven or eight weeks. ▶

Angle perm. Instead of using perming rods, the hair is wound on to flat, plastic rectangles. Many salons use old colorant tubes split, cleaned and flattened. This produces angular kinks which give an unusual tousled effect. ▶

Weave perm. A tail comb (see page 24) is woven in and out of sections of hair, separating a few strands from each. These strands are permed, and the rest left straight. ▶

This produces random curls which give the resulting style added body and an unusual texture.

Corkscrew perm. The hair is wound on to corkscrew-shaped perming rods. Alternatively, the hair can be wound in a spiral around the length of normal perming rods, and angled vertically on the head. The finished look is a mass of ringlets. ▶

Root perm. For this perm, only the roots of the hair are permed. The hair is divided into sections, and the ends wrapped tightly in pieces of plastic wrap to protect them from the solution. The resulting height and fullness create a dramatic effect. ▶

Pin curl perm. The hair is divided into small sections. One section is wound around a finger. The hair is then released, and the curl clipped flat against the head. This is repeated until the head is covered in curls. Finally, a perm is applied. The result is soft, natural-looking waves. ▶

Dos and don'ts when perming

★ Do choose a perm which is pH balanced (see page 42).

★ Do test the client's skin first (see page 34).

★ Don't perm hair more than once every four months.

★ Don't perm streaked hair, as the perm won't work evenly.

★ Don't perm hair which is out of condition.

Straightening hair

Straightening curly hair is far more risky than perming straight hair. This is because the process stretches the hair shaft, and unless it is done by an experienced professional, the hair could break off. This is the safest method:

1. Apply perming solution to the hair, avoiding the roots. Leave on for 10-15 minutes. Then divide the hair into four equal sections.

2. Starting with the back left-hand section, comb out a tress about 5mm wide. Put on more perming solution. Then coat it in petroleum jelly (to keep it straight while solution takes effect). Comb it straight again.

3. Continue in the same way until you have finished the section. then do the same with the remaining three sections. Leave for a further 10-15 minutes.

4. Apply neutralizer, as for a perm. Leave on for around 10 minutes*. Rinse, shampoo and condition the hair, keeping it as straight as possible throughout. Then style it in the usual way.

Check the packet for guidelines.

Careers in hairdressing

There is a wide variety of exciting career opportunities within the world of hairdressing. These range from salon work or teaching to modelling or session styling.

For some careers, professional qualifications are essential: for others, experience and enthusiasm count for more. Here you can find out about some of the jobs within the hairdressing industry.

Salon hairdresser

Description: cutting clients' hair within a salon or barber's shop.

Qualifications: apprenticeship and/or formal qualifications (see pages 22-23).

Personal qualities: a good eye for detail and a sense of line and form. The ability to get on well with people and communicate your ideas clearly is also essential. Private schools also look for a good basic education.

Getting started: enrol at a college, reputable private school or academy. Alternatively, enquire about apprenticeships on leaving school (your school's career advisor should be able to help you).

Salon manager

Description: responsible for all aspects of running a salon, from making sure it is profitable to training and supervising staff.

Qualifications: none essential, but you are unlikely to succeed without some years' experience of working in a salon. A business management course is useful.

Personal qualities: business sense, good communication skills, confidence, the ability to motivate and handle staff and generate team spirit.

Getting started: work in a salon and watch the day-to-day running of it. Apply for courses in business and salon management.

Teacher

Description: teaching students of hairdressing at a college or within a private hairdressing school or academy.

Qualifications: good formal qualifications (see page 23) and experience in the hairdressing industry. You will also need a teaching diploma if working in a college.

Personal qualities: a love of hairdressing and an awareness of its trends. Enthusiasm, patience and the ability to communicate.

Getting started: build up qualifications and experience. Learn teaching skills by watching the ways others teach you.

Session stylist

Description: Styling models' hair for photographic sessions or fashion shows and demonstrations.

Qualifications: none essential, but most stylists move from salon work into session styling.

Personal qualities: good fashion sense, imagination, an eye for detail, energy, diplomacy and an ability to communicate your ideas.

Getting started: build up a portfolio (a file) of photographs of hair you have styled. You may get a chance to do this by working as an assistant to an established stylist or photographer. There are also photographic courses available which will give you a good insight into the field of hairdressing for photography.

Coloring/perming technician

Description: developing new ideas and techniques in coloring and/or perming for a large salon. Creating original looks for fashion shows and demonstrations.

Qualifications: good basic education, a formal hairdressing qualification and additional coloring and/or perming qualifications.

Personal qualities: a good understanding of scientific theory, strong color sense, artistic flair and an ability to respond quickly and imaginatively to new trends.

Getting started: train as a hairdresser. Then take specific and advanced courses in coloring and/or perming whenever possible. Acquire experience within the salon.

Demonstrator

Description: working for a large hair products company demonstrating and selling their new ranges to various clients.

Qualifications: should be a competent hairdresser who can perform well in public.

Personal qualities: a lively and outgoing personality as you will be dealing with a lot of different people. Enthusiasm and a liking for being on the move as the work also involves a lot of travelling.

Getting started: a basic hairdressing qualification (see pages 22-23) and some practical hairdressing experience is usually required by companies recruiting hair product demonstrators.

Hairdressing for television, film and theatre*

Description: styling hair for actors or television presenters. You will often work from drawings or be required to create styles from specific periods in history.

Qualifications: a good basic education. Proven ability in history and art is helpful, and sometimes essential in television. Make-up skills are often required for television.

Personal qualities: accuracy and attention to detail, tact when dealing with people, a liking for travel, stamina and adaptability as jobs may come up at very short notice and at different locations.

Getting started: some television companies train their own hairdressing and make-up staff, so apply direct to them. For film and theatre, first get a formal qualification (see pages 22-23) before applying to companies.

Ship's hairdresser

Description: working on board a cruise liner as the resident hairdresser.

Qualifications: good formal qualifications (see page 23). You will also need to have experience in related fields such as make-up, hair-removal and manicuring.

Personal qualities: the ability to adapt to long periods at sea, self-reliance, good communication skills, enthusiasm and patience.

Getting started: build up hairdressing and beautician experience (for example, you can apply for additional beauty courses whilst working within a salon). Then apply direct to the major cruise companies.

Public relations and marketing consultant

Description: providing publicity and up-to-date information about hairdressers, hair product manufacturers and retailers to the press and potential customers.

Qualifications: none essential, however many companies do insist on a good basic education. Some business studies courses include public relations and marketing as an additional option.

Personal qualities: business sense, good communication skills, tact and initiative.

Getting started: apply for courses in public relations and marketing or business study courses which offer these as a part of training. Alternatively, apply for any kind of job within a marketing or public relations company in order to gain experience. Some companies are also willing to recruit experienced professional hairdressers.

Wigmaker

Description: making wigs for private clients or for television, theatre or film productions.

Qualifications: a formal qualification in hairdressing and/or wigmaking. Many employers also insist that you carry out further training within the company.

Personal qualities: good manual skills, co-ordination, dedication and patience.

Getting started: start with a basic formal qualification, then apply to wig-making companies. Some television companies also employ wig-makers, however, you will need to have gained some experience before you apply to them for work.

Modelling

Description: Modelling hairstyles and clothes for shows or photographs. It is very unusual to specialise only in modelling hairstyles.

Qualifications: none. There are modelling courses available, however unless you have the looks they are a waste of time.

Personal qualities: Healthy hair and good looks. A model also needs patience, good humour, energy and the ability to communicate.

Boys must be at least 1.78m tall, with a medium build, good looks and hair. They must start their career between the ages of 16 and 22.

Girls must be between 1.73m and 1.78m tall and take size 10** or 12** clothes. Good looks, clear skin and well-kept hair are essential. Girls must start their career between the ages of 16 and 20.

Getting started: Most regular models are chosen through agencies. Send a full length photograph and a close-up head and shoulder shot of yourself to a number of reputable agencies. Write your name, age, height and size on the back and enclose a stamped self-addressed envelope. To gain some experience you could enquire about modelling at a local hairdressing school or salon for their demonstrations or shows.

Warning

There are an infinite number of modelling courses on offer, all of which charge a fee. Some are of a high standard, and offer good value for money. Others are overpriced and have little to offer.
 Always shop around before committing yourself, and check that it is recognized by your local education authority. If possible, ask advice from someone who has already completed the course.

---

* You will need union recognition to work in these areas.
** European size 38, US size 8; European size 40, US size 10.

Hair charts

Over the next five pages you will find charts telling you, at a glance, everything you need to know about hair care and styling products (such as shampoos and mousses), hair colorants, and styling equipment (such as crimpers and diffusers). There is also information on common hair problems, their causes and how to treat them.

Shampoo	Properties	Comments
For greasy hair	Contains a high proportion of detergent which strips the scalp of excess grease.	Large amounts or over-use can over-dry your scalp, causing it to flake.
For normal hair	Contains an average proportion of detergent. Cleans your hair without affecting the natural flow of oil.	The milder the better - look for products that are pH balanced (see right).
For dry hair	Contains a lower proportion of detergent - has added moisturiser. This prevents drying of the scalp and hair shaft.	Look for one with a protein or oil-enriched moisturiser.
Mild or frequent-wash	Very mild formula. Gentle on the scalp.	Recommended for all hair types. Often better for your hair than specially formulated shampoos.
Herbal	Contains extracts of various herbs and plants.	Available for all hair types – there are specific herbs for different hair conditions.
Henna	Conditions your hair and strengthens its natural color.	Continuous use may eventually dull your hair.
Colorfast	Contains little detergent. Similar to mild or frequent-wash shampoos. Prevents dyed hair from fading.	Not very effective on greasy hair.
Anti-dandruff	Contains the chemicals zinc pyrithione and selenium sulphide to slow down cell division in the scalp.	Over-use dries and dulls your hair. Alternate with your usual shampoo.
Insecticidal	Contains the chemicals malathion or carbaryl. These kill head lice.	Very harsh. Use conditioner after each treatment. You can also buy special combs which remove lice eggs.
Dry	Powder made with talcum powder or cornstarch. Absorbs oil and dirt when brushed through hair.	Takes time to remove all traces of powder. Over-use can dull your hair.
Medicated	Contains antiseptic to kill bacteria on the scalp.	Not effective on dandruff.
Silicone-based	Contains in-built conditioner.	More expensive, but saves buying conditioner.

What is a pH factor?

You may have noticed that some shampoos state their pH factor. A pH factor indicates the concentration of hydrogen in a solution. This tells you whether a substance is alkaline or acid based, as the more hydrogen there is in a substance the more alkaline it is.

The pH scale

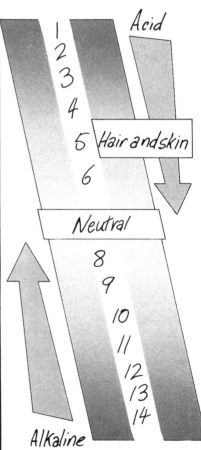

Your skin and hair have an acid content (a pH balance of 4.5-5.5). You should therefore look for products that have a similar acid balance (ideally a pH balance of 5) as these are better for your hair.

Conditioner	Properties	How to apply	Comments
Conditioning rinse	Light protein-enriched liquid that penetrates the hair shaft and strengthens it.	Leave it on your hair for about 2-3 minutes before rinsing.	Rinses away easily. Especially good for greasy hair.
Oil or cream-based balsams	Coats the hair shaft in a thin film of wax or oil, making it shiny and easy to manage.	Can be washed out immediately.	Particularly effective on thick, dry hair.
Henna wax	A thick, clear wax which leaves hair shiny and manageable.	Mix with hot water and leave on dry hair for 30 minutes.	Effective on all hair types.
Hot oil	Olive or almond oil coats the hair shaft, repairing damaged cuticles.	Warm the oil and massage into hair. Leave for as long as possible.	Particularly good for dry or damaged hair.

Hair colorant	Types available	How it works	How to apply	Durability	Comments
Temporary	Wash-in/wash-out shampoos, gels, mousses, crayons, sprays, brush-on paints, cream	Coats the hair shaft with a fine film of color.	Apply on clean, damp hair and leave to dry.	Washes out after one shampoo, or a little longer if hair is porous*.	Safe to use at home. Temporary colors do not color grey hair.
Semi-permanent	Coloring conditioner, shampoos, mousses, creams, liquids	Penetrates and colors the cuticle.	Apply on clean damp hair. Leave, for 10-20 minutes then rinse away.	4-6 weeks	Leaves hair shiny and bouncy. Will not lighten hair. Partially effective on grey hair. Over-use can dull hair.
Permanent	Liquid or cream and separate container of hydrogen peroxide (liquid chemical)	Penetrates and changes the natural color in the cortex.	Mix together the two components then apply to dry hair.	Grows out. Roots need re-touching every 4 weeks.	Good for grey hair. Too risky to try at home: should be done professionally. Dries the hair.
Bleach	Powder, paste, oil, liquid or cream; plus container of hydrogen peroxide	Penetrates the cortex and removes color from hair.	Mix together the two components and apply on dry hair.	Grows out. Roots need re-touching every 4 weeks.	Colors hair blond only. Must be done professionally.
Lighteners	Rinses or sprays	Acts in the same way as bleach (see above). Contains peroxide.	Apply on dry or damp hair. Many use the sun or heat to activate them.	Grows out. Roots need re-touching every 4 weeks.	Combination of peroxide and sunlight or heat can damage hair.
Metallic	Lotion or rinse	Contains lead or silver salts that slowly change color after several applications.	Apply on dry hair.	Grows out. Roots must be re-touched every 4 weeks.	Deposits left by the salts can damage your hair, leaving it dry and brittle.
Vegetable (Henna)	Powder	Penetrates and stains the cuticle and some of the cortex.	Mix with warm water to form paste. Then apply to damp hair.	Fades gradually.	Safe to apply at home, but very messy. May dull hair if used too often.

This means that the hair shaft can be easily penetrated.

Styling products	Form	How to apply	Uses	Comments
Gel	Transparent jelly. Comes in jars, tubs and tubes.	Apply to the roots first and spread through dry or damp hair. Style with fingertips.	Keeps hair in position. Wet-look gel moulds hair close to the head and keeps it firmly in position.	Messy to apply. Invisible when dry (unless wet-look). If your hair is fine, use gel only on the roots.
Mousse	Comes in a pump dispenser. Has the consistency of shaving foam.	Apply to the roots of damp hair. Comb through evenly.	Holds style in place and gives it body.	Particularly effective on curly or wavy hair. Conditioning mousses are best.
Glaze	Comes as a gel in tubes.	Apply to towel-dried hair then style as normal.	Keeps hair firmly in place. Dries hard and adds shine and body to hair.	Particularly good for slicking back unruly hair. Hair needs to be styled carefully as once dry, glaze holds firm.
Grease	Comes in tubs and jars.	Apply on wet or dry hair. Either smooth on with hands or comb through.	Holds hair in place. Large quantities produce a slicked-back look.	Messy to apply. Leaves hair sticky to touch. Good for imitating fifties styles.
Setting lotion	Colorless liquid. Comes in a bottle.	Sprinkle on to towel-dried hair. Comb through and style as normal.	Adds body and keeps hair in place when dry. Use with rollers, or when a firm hold is required.	Particularly good for fine hair. Can be rather messy to apply. Leaves hair a little hard to the touch.
Blow drying lotion	Colorless liquid. Comes in a bottle.	Sprinkle on to hair before blow drying.	Similar to a setting lotion, but gives hair a softer look and feel.	Particularly good for straight, sleek cuts. Many contain a chemical which protects hair from heat.
Hairspray	Fine, quick-drying varnish which comes in an aerosol or pump dispenser.	Spray on to styled hair, from a distance of at least 20cm.	Holds finished style in place.	Use sparingly. Brushes out. Dries hair if left in too long.
Finishing spray	Light oil. Comes in aerosol or pump dispensers.	Spray on to styled hair.	Makes hair look healthy and shiny.	Particularly effective on sleek styles and slick-backed looks.
Hair gloss	Gel or oil-based. Comes in jars and tubs.	Smooth evenly through damp hair.	Keeps styled hair in place and makes it look shiny.	Gel-based gloss provides a stronger hold. Oil-based gloss is particularly good for making Afro hair shiny.
Moisturiser	Comes as cream in jars and tubs or sprays in aerosols or pump dispensers.	Apply to hair before styling.	Makes hair soft and shiny and helps loosen any tangles.	Particularly useful for conditioning Afro hair.

Styling equipment	Description	Uses	What to look for	Comments
Brush	Available in different types such as vent, styling and radial (see page 24).	For brushing and styling dry hair only.	Look for natural or synthetic bristles with rounded ends.	Wash regularly. Check bristles by pressing them into your palm; if they hurt they are too sharp.
Comb	Available with close or wide-set teeth (or both combined).	For styling and untangling wet or dry hair.	Choose wide-toothed synthetic combs with rounded ends.	Wash regularly in shampoo and warm water. Never use metal combs as they tear the hair.
Hairdryer	Hand-held, electrically-powered drying tool.	For blow drying hair.	Look for one with several temperature settings and a nozzle attachment to diffuse the heat.	Alway use on a low temperature setting, and hold at least 10cm from the hair.
Rollers	Small plastic or foam cylinders, held in place by clips.	For curling and perming hair.	Choose ribbed or fabric covered rollers rather than the spiky sort.	Store them in a clean bag or box.
Styling rods	Flexible foam, rubber or fabric-covered wires.	For curling and perming hair.	Check the ones you buy are very bendy. Choose good quality fabric ones if you are leaving them in overnight.	Create a softer look than rollers.
Heated rollers	Rollers which are electrically or steam-heated in a special container before use.	For curling hair quickly.	Look for rollers with a smooth surface. Choose steam-heated ones if you intend to use them often.	Over-use may make hair dry, especially at the ends.
Heated styling rods	Styling rods which are electrically-heated before use in a special container.	For curling hair quickly.	Choose very flexible ones covered in good quality foam or rubber.	Better for your hair than conventional heated rollers as you do not need clips to secure them.
Crimpers	Two thermostatically-controlled plates with crinkly surfaces, between which the hair is pressed.	Makes hair crinkly.	Choose crimpers that are lightweight and easy to handle.	Use on conditoned hair. Do not brush crimped hair.
Straighteners	Two thermostatically-controlled flat plates between which the hair is pressed.	Straighten curly or wavy hair.	Choose straighteners which are lightweight and easy to handle.	Do not use too often. Do not brush your hair once it has been straightened.
Curling irons	Hand-held, cylindrical hinged clamp which is electrically or steam-heated.	For curling hair quickly.	Choose steam-heated irons, as they are better for your hair.	Do not use too often. Start with the irons right at the ends of your hair, to avoid kinks.
Heated brush	Electrically or steam-heated radial brush.	For curling hair quickly.	Look for retractable bristles. These prevent the hair from tangling when the brush is removed.	Do not use too often. Once curled, it is best to style the hair with your fingers or a comb.

Styling equipment	Description	Uses	What to look for	Comments
Scissors	Hairdressing scissors are specially designed for the purpose (see page 24).	For cutting hair.	Choose very sharp, lightweight ones. Short blades will give you more control.	It is worth spending the money to get really good quality scissors.
Diffuser	Large round nozzle attachment for hairdryer which spreads air-flow more widely.	Dries hair gently and steadily without blowing it around.	Make sure you buy one which fits your make and size of dryer.	Good for styling curly or wavy hair. Can only be bought through trade outlets.
Clippers	Small hand-held electrically operated razor.	Cuts hair very close to the head.	Look for lightweight clippers with sharp blades.	Only use clippers if you are professionally qualified. Take care not to nip the skin.

Hair problem	Symptoms	Causes	Solutions
Dandruff	Itchy scalp, white flakes in hair and dropping onto shoulders.	The cells of the skin multiply too quickly and the dead cells build up and flake off. May be stress-related.	Can be controlled, but not cured. Alternate between your normal shampoo and an anti-dandruff shampoo. Resist the temptation to scratch your scalp.
Split ends (Fragilitas crinium)	Hair has dull, frizzy appearance as small ends stick out.	The end of the hair shaft splits in two because the hair has worn out, or is damaged by heated appliances, chemicals or harsh brushing.	Have hair trimmed regularly.
Hair breaking	Hair feels brittle and is dull in appearance. Tends to break off in clumps while brushing and combing.	Usually self-inflicted, through using harsh chemicals, heated appliances, brushing too vigorously, pulling hair into tight styles or using rubber bands.	Use fabric-covered bands to tie hair up. Avoid harsh treatments and heated appliances. Never rub or tug hair.
Static	When brushed, hair stands out and crackles. Difficult to style and looks dull.	Cuticles of each hair may have been damaged so that they are rough instead of smooth. Rough or dry hairs rub against each other and produce static when brushed.	Use a light conditioner which smooths the cuticle and neutralizes the electrical charge.
Head lice	Very itchy scalp. Examining the scalp under a good light reveals lice and white egg sacks.	Contact with another afflicted person.*	Use an insecticidal shampoo prescribed by your doctor and follow the instructions carefully. Ask all members of your family to use it too, as lice spread easily.
Grey hair	Hair appears grey in color (individual hairs are in fact white – it is the mixture of white and natural color that gives an illusion of grey).	Grey hair has no color pigment in the cortex (see page 4). It can be caused by shock, illness, stress or ageing.	Disguise grey hair by coloring it to match the rest of your hair.

Lice breed in clean hair. Anyone can become infected, so there is no need to feel embarrassed.

Going further

If you would like to find out about any aspect of hairdressing, the books and selected contact addresses listed below will give you a good starting point.

Book list

General

African Hairstyles: Styles of Yesterday and Today
Esi Sagay
Heinemann

An Illustrated Dictionary of Hairdressing and Wigmaking
James Stevens Fox
Batsford

Fashions in Hair: The First Five Thousand Years
Richard Carson
Peter Owen
(distributed in the US & Canada by Dufour Editions Inc.)

The Miriam Stoppard Health & Beauty Book
Dorling Kindersley
(not available in the US or Canada)

Hair Matters
Joshua & Daniel Galvin
MacMillan
(not available in the US or Canada)

Hair Care: Deborah McCormick
The Body Shop Book
MacDonald

Vogue Guide to Hair Care
Felicity Clark
Penguin

Career

Becoming a Hairdresser
Pauline Wheatley
Batsford

Coloring: a salon handbook
Lesley Hatton
Blackwell
(distributed in the US by BSP Inc. and in Canada by OUP)

Science for Hairdressing Students
(3rd edition)
Lee & Inglis
Pergamon Press

Working in Hairdressing
Marina Thaine & Robert Griffin
Batsford

Cutting Hair the Vidal Sassoon Way
(2nd edition)
William Heinemann

Cutting and Styling: A Salon Handbook
Hatton & Hatton
Collins
(distributed in the US by BSP Inc. and in Canada by OUP)

Hygiene: A Salon Handbook
Philip Hatton
Blackwell
(distributed in the US by BSP Inc. and in Canada by OUP)

Mastering Hairdressing
Leo Palladino
MacMillan Masters Series
(not available in the US or Canada)

Perming & Straightening: A Salon Handbook
Hatton & Hatton
Blackwell
(distributed in the US by BSP Inc. and in Canada by OUP)

Useful addresses

UK

British Association of Professional Hairdresser Employers
1a Barbon Close
Great Ormond Street
London WC1 3JX

City and Guilds of London Institute
46 Britannia Street
London WC1X 9RG

Hairdressing Training Board
Silver House Silver Street
Doncaster DN1 1HL

The Guild of Hairdressers
24 Woodbridge Road
Guildford
Surrey GU1 1DY

The Hairdressing Council
12 David House
45 High Street
South Norwood
London SE25 6HJ

Vidal Sassoon School of Hairdressing
56-58 Davies Mews
London
W1Y 1AS

Vidal Sassoon Education Centre
19-21 King Street
Manchester

Australia

Hairdressing and Beauty Industry Association
1202 Toorak Road
Hartwell Victoria
Australia 3125

New Zealand

New Zealand Council of Ladies Hairdressing Associations
PO Box 28-322
Auckland 5

US

National Association of Cosmetologists
3510 Olive Street
St Louis
Mo 63103

Vidal Sassoon Academy & School of Cosmetology
1222 Santa Monica Mall
California 90401

Canada

National Canadian Hairdressers & Cosmetologists Association Incorporated
1982 Islington Avenue
Weston
Ontario M9P 3N5

Vidal Sassoon Educational Center
37 Avenue Road
Toronto M5R 2G3

Index

Acknowledgements

The following photographers and modelling agencies generously allowed us to reproduce their work –

Photographers: Robyn Beeche, Tim Bret-Day, Peter Brown, Marc Bucklow, Peter Calvin, Roger Eaton, Karen Elmers, Martin Evening, Melissa Halstead, Christian Hartman, Stevie Hughes, Mark Lewis, James Martin, Jean Pierre Masclet, Eamonn J McCabe, Al McDonald, Stephen Murphy, Mike Owen, Malcolm Pasley, Jonathan Rea, David Schienmann.

Agencies: Askews, Bookings, Count Eight, Edit, Folio, Freddies, Gavins, Laraine Ashton, Look, Marco Rasala, Models One Elite, Models One Men, Nevs, Premier, Review, Select, Storm, Synchro, Take Two, Unique, Will Dells, Ziggy.

First published in 1988 by Usborne Publishing Ltd, 20 Garrick Street, London WC2E 9BJ, England.

The name Usborne and the device ♈ are Trade Marks of Usborne Publishing Ltd. All rights reserved.

Haircare Limited is the sole and exclusive licensee of Richardson-Vicks Inc and Proctor & Gamble Ltd within the United Kingdom of Great Britain and all rights are hereby reserved. No part of this publication may be reproduced or transmitted, in any form or by any means, electronic, mechanical, photocopying, recording or otherwise, or stored in any retrieval system of any nature without the written permission of the copyright holders and the publisher, application for which shall be made to the publisher.

Printed in Belgium   American edition 1989.